D1461494

FESTIVE WIT

First published in 2006 by

PRION
an imprint of the
Carlton Publishing Group
20 Mortimer Street
London W1T 3JW

2 4 6 8 10 9 7 5 3 1

Introduction and selection copyright © Holly Robinson 2006
Design copyright © Carlton Publishing Group 2006

A catalogue record for this book is available from the British Library.

ISBN-10: 1-85375-604-0
ISBN-13: 978-1-85375-604-7

Typeset by E-Type
Printed in Great Britain
by Mackays

FESTIVE WIT

For When the Christmas Season Gets Too Much to Bear

Compiled by Holly Robinson

Contents

What Christmas Means to Me

Christmas: A day set apart and consecrated to gluttony, drunkenness, maudlin sentiment, gift-taking, public dullness and domestic behaviour.

Ambrose Bierce

Christmas is the glorious time of great Too-Much.

Leigh Hunt

The whole point of Christmas is that it is a debauch, as it was probably long before the birth of Christ was arbitrarily fixed at that date.

George Orwell

Christmas … a time of peace, harmony, sickly sentimentality, high kitsch and grotesque opportunism; a time when families come together, when thoughts turn to loved ones far away, when sleigh bells ring and chestnuts roast on an open fire, when the red red robin comes bob-bob-bobbin' along …

Mick Brown

It was about Santa Claus and elves and stockings hung by the fireplace and good cheer and a big dinner and sugar cookies and gifts, gifts, and more gifts.

Binnie Kirshenbaum

… that seasonal festival that involves deceiving small children; eating chocolate in irritating bell shapes before 7 a.m.; corridor creeping; paying to sit on some bearded weirdo's knee; lying enthusiastically about pot-pourri gift

What Christmas Means to Me

sets; watching a James Bond you've seen thrice before;
turning off the Queen; rolling up at church once a year,
drunk; eating turkey (a substance also found in Twizzlers);
heartburn; passive-aggressive family conversations; and
hiding from relatives at Marks & Spencer's refunds counter.

Kate Muir

The sulker's Mount Everest.

*Christopher Douglas and Mick Newman, Mastering
the Universe radio show*

Christmas is wishing there really was such a thing as an old-
fashioned Christmas.

Charles M. Schulz

Christmas is a time which can be lonely, can be sad, but it
can also bring joy, laughter and light, and a time of great
blessings to so many.

Diana, Princess of Wales

What is Christmas if not the season to be greedy? Isn't that
the whole point? Look at the carols: 'Bring us some figgy
pudding', 'Bring me flesh and bring me wine' – it's all
gimme gimme gimme.

Giles Conran

It was the season of hospitality, merriment, and open-
heartedness ...

Charles Dickens

Christmas is a time for saying that Christmas is a time for
doing things that one should, frankly, be doing anyway.
'Christmas is a time for considering people less fortunate
than ourselves.' Oh, July and August aren't, is that it?
'Christmas is a time for forgiveness.' We should be
vindictive and beastly for the rest of the year?

Stephen Fry

What Christmas Means to Me

I don't hold that Christmas is 'all about togetherness' – it's all about watching telly and having impressively resonant wind.

Caitlin Moran

Christmas is a time when people of all religions come together to worship Jesus Christ.

Bart Simpson, The Simpsons

Christmas is the Christian's Christmas present to everyone else. Christmas, for a Christian, tells us why people matter.

Dr Rowan Williams, Archbishop of Canterbury

I've got a family and children and the best part of it is giving presents. It's also the time of year when I can replenish my socks and ties.

A. C. Grayling

Christmas is hell in a stupid sweater.

Carina Chocano

Christmas – that magic blanket that wraps itself about us, that something so intangible it is like a fragrance.

Augusta E. Rundel

Xmas, *n.*: Popular festival made to sound like a skin disease.

Mike Barfield

Christmas is that magical time of the year when all your money disappears.

Hal Roach

Christmas is the season for kindling the fire of hospitality in the hall, the genial flame of charity in the heart.

Washington Irving

What Christmas Means to Me

Christmas is not in tinsel and lights and outward show. The secret lies in an inner glow. It's lighting a fire inside the heart … It's a glorious dream in the soul of man.

Wilford A. Peterson

Aren't we forgetting the true meaning of Christmas – the birth of Santa?

Bart Simpson, The Simpsons

Tradition. That's what you associate with Christmas: tradition. And drink-driving. And despair and loneliness. And Argos. But mainly tradition.

Charlie Brooker

Christmas is about food, warmth, family, friends, goodwill and the aspiration to be better. Christmas, like religion, is a human instinct in the face of darkness.

Stephen Pile

Christmas is not an external event at all, but a piece of one's home that one carries in one's heart.

Freya Stark

Christmas is a box of tree ornaments that have become part of the family.

Charles M. Schulz

Christmas – whose delights are 95 per cent anticipation …

Valerie Grove

Christmas, my child, is love in action … Every time we love, every time we give, it's Christmas.

Dale Evans Rogers

Dickensian Christmas: Costumed Rotarians may approach you in the street for money and won't take 'sod Victorian values' for an answer.

Malcolm Burgess

What Christmas Means to Me

Yule offers plastic robins and alloy trees, advocaat and mince bricks, 'A Christmas Carol' and 'White Christmas', smutty cards and bogus bonhomie ... and drunken Santas and cotton snow.

Alan Coren

What is Christmas? It is tenderness for the past, courage for the present, hope for the future.

Agnes N. Pahro

Christmas is a holiday in which neither the past nor the future is as of much interest as the present.

Anon

I do know that Christmas is more, much more, than the exchange of gifts, the merriment round the table, the carols however truly beautiful ... Whatever Christmas means to us, from nothing to everything, it will last for ever. And love, the beloved republic, may weep, but will abide.

Bernard Levin

Christmas, to me, is a place where I wish time itself would stand still and embrace us all, for ever, in that feeling of love, security and happiness.

Toyah Willcox

But I am sure I have always thought of Christmas time, when it came round – apart from the veneration due to its sacred name and origin, if anything belonging to it can be apart from that – as a good time, a kind, forgiving, charitable, pleasant time – and I say, God bless it!

Charles Dickens

'Tis The Season to be Jolly: Christmas Spirit

I'm a fool for Christmas. Stick a bit of holly on it, and I'm there.

Amanda Craig

I love Christmas ... When you picture December, don't you just see it by candlelight? I love the fellowship and the food, I love the anticipation. It's cold skin and velvet and quick, puffy snows. I love the frenzy – in kitchens and restaurants and malls, even. You know 'tis really the season when you can't seem to locate your car. I love that it all starts in September ... We walk faster and think faster and do more more more until we do ourselves into a stupor. Then we eat too much and give ourselves stuff and finally take a day off.

Carolyn Hax

Christmas waves a magic wand over this world, and behold, everything is softer and more beautiful.

Norman Vincent Peale

We love it, every little bit of it. Robins sitting on spades, a Christmas tree that would make a Mountie homesick, chestnuts exploding into thousands of little pieces in the fireplace, snow, tinsel, holly dripping with scarlet berries, even that terrible moment when you know that, to put your cracker hat on, you're going to have to split it because your head's too big!

Phillip Schofield

A lovely thing about Christmas is that it's compulsory, like a thunderstorm, and we all go through it together.

Garrison Keillor

'Tis The Season to be Jolly

I'm so riddled with the holiday season that the mere
mention of a stocking filler sexually arouses me.

John Waters

I love everything about Christmas. I savour the opening of
each little door of my Advent calendar (what's wrong with
having an Advent calendar at the age of 36?). I usually burst
into tears when I see the town centre Christmas lights for
the first time and my favourite sound in the world is our
old wind-up Nativity scene which plays 'Silent Night' at an
ever-decreasing pace.

Mel Giedroyc

Before I give myself over to Christmas goodwill, I am
making a list of the people whom I would like to murder.
Every day I collect a few more and I am knitting their
descriptions into a huge purple stocking.

Janet Hills

Christmas is about a child, and for children: like
parenthood, if you don't throw yourself into it body and
soul you will have a wretched time.

Amanda Craig

Mr Andy Park, a milkman-turned-electrician from
Melksham in Wiltshire … is so entranced with the
trappings of Yuletide … he has, he claims, lived every single
day as if it were December 25th for the past twelve and a
half years – and has the paunch and moon-face to prove it.
Since he says he starts a new turkey each day … this must
mean in the past twelve years Andy has got through 4,478
turkeys. That's not to mention 26,280 roast potatoes, 30,660
stuffing balls, 219,000 mushy peas, 109,500 sprouts, 6,200
carrots and 2,190 pints of gravy, as well as 4,478 Christmas
puddings, 87,600 mince pies and 4,478 bottles of wine.

Victoria Moore

'Tis The Season to be Jolly

I absolutely love Christmas … I've spent about £250,000 in total celebrating Christmas every day for the past twelve years. I've also got through 36 ovens and 42 video recorders by watching the Queen's speech every day as well as Christmas films.

Andy Park, a.k.a. 'Mr Christmas'

Christmas is not a time or a season but a state of mind. To cherish peace and goodwill, to be plenteous in mercy, is to have the real spirit of Christmas. If we think on these things, there will be born in us a Saviour and over us will shine a star sending its gleam of hope to the world.

Calvin Coolidge

Still xmas is a good time with all those presents and good food and i hope it will never die out or at any rate not until i am grown up and hav to pay for it all.

Geoffrey Willans and Ronald Searle, 'How to be Topp',
The Compleet Molesworth

To perceive Christmas through its wrappings becomes more difficult each year.

E. B. White

There are some people who want to throw their arms round you simply because it is Christmas; there are other people who want to strangle you simply because it is Christmas.

Robert Lynd

I'll be spending a typical American Christmas. My tree is from Canada, the ornaments from Hong Kong. The lights come from Japan – and the idea from Bethlehem!

Robert Orben

'Tis The Season to be Jolly

Whether or not we watch *The Sound of Music* from California, we do eat an American bird, stuffed with Spanish chestnuts, garlanded with potatoes from the New World, sprouts from Brussels, a plum pudding spiced from the Orient, and we sit around an alien tree, and sing with music from Sweden about a King of Bohemia, the one who looked out on St Stephen's Day. And that other favourite carol, the one that interrupts many a silent night, is as British as sauerkraut and bratwurst.

Anthony Smith

The Xmas holidays have this high value: that they remind Forgetters of the Forgotten, and repair damaged relationships.

Mark Twain

The holidays are welcome to me partly because they are such rallying points for the affections which get so much thrust aside in the business and preoccupations of daily life.

George E. Woodberry

Christmas is awesome. First of all you get to spend time with people you love. Secondly, you can get drunk and no one can say anything. Third you give presents. What's better than giving presents? And fourth, getting presents. So four things. Not bad for one day. It's really the greatest day of all time.

Michael Scott, The Office (USA)

Now that nobody believes in God, or Santa Claus, or the spirit of giving, or family values, or snow, or the whoppers that supermarkets tell us about where they get their turkeys, or sending cards, or the monarchy, or old people, or magic or home baking, there is very little left of Christmas but ritual.

Giles Coren

'Tis The Season to be Jolly

The only real blind person at Christmastime is he who has not Christmas in his heart.

Helen Keller

It is Christmas in the heart that puts Christmas in the air.

W. T. Ellis

About this time of year I get a burst of what my family calls, glumly, That Xmas Feeling. No orange is safe from a rash of cloves; my husband groans as I hammer another nail into the woodwork to support swathes of cards, and my devoutly atheist children put fingers in ears as Christmas carols play more or less on a loop.

Amanda Craig

– Merry Christmas, Charlie Brown. At this time of year I think we should put aside all our differences and try to be kind.
– Why does it have to be just for this time of year? Can't it be all year 'round?
– What are you? Some kind of fanatic or something?

Lucy and Charlie Brown, A Charlie Brown Christmas

My philosophy? Eat the icing! Light those expensive candles! Use those pretty little soaps! Wear, use, and enjoy! There's no time more important than NOW! Happy holidays.

Erma Bombeck

Christmas is coming,
The geese are getting fat,
Please to put a penny
In the old man's hat.
If you haven't got a penny,
A ha'penny will do,
If you haven't got a ha'penny,
Then God bless you!

English nursery rhyme

I truly believe that if we keep telling the Christmas story, singing the Christmas songs, and living the Christmas spirit, we can bring joy and happiness and peace to this world.

Norman Vincent Peale

That's the true spirit of Christmas: people being helped by people other than me.

Jerry Seinfeld, Seinfeld

I sometimes think we expect too much of Christmas Day. We try to crowd into it the long arrears of kindliness and humanity of the whole year. As for me, I like to take my Christmas a little at a time, all through the year. And thus I drift along into the holidays – let them overtake me unexpectedly – waking up some fine morning and suddenly saying to myself, 'Why, this is Christmas Day!'

David Grayson

I wish we could put some of the Christmas spirit in jars and open a jar of it every month.

Harlan Miller

The Christmas spirit that goes out with the dried-up Christmas tree is just as worthless.

Anon

At Christmas play and make good cheer,
For Christmas comes but once a year.

Thomas Tusser

I will honour Christmas in my heart, and try to keep it all the year.

Charles Dickens

In the immortal words of Tiny Tim, 'God help us every one!'

Groucho Marx

Unto Us a Child is Born: Traditional Christmas

– Shall I begin the Christmas story?
– Absolutely, as long as it's not that terribly depressing one about the chap who gets born on Christmas Day, shoots his mouth off about everything under the sun, and then comes a cropper with a couple of rum coves on top of a hill in Johnny Arab land.
– You mean Jesus, Sire?
– Yes, that's the fellow. Keep him out of it. He always spoils the Christmas atmos.

Ebenezer Blackadder and George, the Prince Regent, Blackadder's Christmas Carol

My four-year-old daughter Amy and I were discussing the Nativity. She told me baby Jesus had to sleep in a manger in a stable. I asked why baby Jesus had to resort to a stable and she immediately replied: 'Oh, that's easy. There was no room left at the Holiday Inn.'

Keith Young

How our newspapers might have covered the Nativity ...

Headline in the *Daily Mail:* BRANSON SPONSORS VIRGIN BIRTH

Barry Cryer

Unto Us a Child is Born

Headline in the *Independent*: SPARSE QUEUES FOR HEROD'S CHRISTMAS SALE

Willie Rushton

Advert in *Exchange and Mart*: UNWANTED FRANKINCENSE AND MYRRH. WILL SWAP FOR NINTENDO.

Graeme Garden, I'm Sorry I Haven't a Clue radio show

The three wise men sound very generous, but what you've got to remember is that those gifts were joint Christmas and birthday presents.

Jimmy Carr

Three wise men? You must be joking.

Anon

The Supreme Court has ruled they can't have a Nativity scene in Washington, D.C. This wasn't for religious reasons. They couldn't find three wise men and a virgin.

Jay Leno

How is the Italian version of Christmas different? One Mary, one Jesus, and 33 wise guys.

Anon

… Christmas Eve when the church was packed to the doors … Plumping to my knees with split-second timing I would scornfully note how few of these festive communicants knew the service. Most of them didn't even kneel, but sat, head in hand as if they were on the lavatory, this their one spiritual evacuation of the year.

Alan Bennett

Christmas is the Disneyfication of Christianity.

Don Cupitt

Unto Us a Child is Born

If you think Christmas is commercialized, take a peek at Bethlehem. 'The Ninth Station Boutique' and 'The Manger Pizzeria' say it all.

Maureen Lipman

Things I Hate About Christmas: Symbolism, the holly and mistletoe, fir trees with decorations on them, fake snow and so forth; it is all pagan anyway. What does it have to do with Jesus? Santa is really Woden, the old Norse god. Admittedly, the symbolism never gets quite as mixed up as in Tokyo, where they nailed Santas to the cross outside stores in the Ginza, although perhaps that is not such a bad idea after all.

Iain Grant

This being Christmastime ... we Americans need to start thinking of ourselves as citizens of the world first and of any particular country second. After all, Jesus himself was – I don't know if you know this – not an American. If you celebrate Christmas religiously, folks, you pray to a young man from the Middle East who, today, would probably get stopped at the airport.

Bill Maher

Nothing embodies the American idea – *e pluribus unum* – better than the American Christmas. This is genuine multiculturalism: if the worry is separation of church and state, the North American Christmas is surely the most successful separation you could devise – Jesus, Mary and Joseph are for home and church; the great secular trinity of Santa, Rudolph and Frosty are for school and mall.

Mark Steyn

Unto Us a Child is Born

Did you hear that the atheists have produced a Christmas play? It's called 'Coincidence on 34th Street'.

Jay Leno

Jesus never put up a tree and exchanged gifts, or left cookies out for Santa. He never made a harried last-minute trip to the mall, or spent Christmas Eve cursing at a toy that he couldn't put together. He celebrated Passover. So, if you want to be more like Jesus, pass the matzo.

Drew Carey

Roses are red
Violets are bluish
If it weren't for Christmas
We'd all be Jewish.

Benny Hill

Nobody does Christmas like the Jews.

Tracy Ullman

… as is often the way with converts and infidels, we celebrated Christmas with all the hoopla as if we were to the manger born.

Binnie Kirshenbaum

Oy to the world.

Frasier Crane, Frasier

I'm Jewish but I only go to temple twice a year: Christmas and Easter.

Jeffrey Ross

December 25th is National Jews Go to the Movies Day.

Jon Stewart

Oh, jeez, why are we talking about God and religion? It's Christmas!

Jackie Harris, Roseanne

Happy Holidays! Politically Correct Christmas

In the old days, it was not called the Holiday Season; the Christians called it 'Christmas' and went to church; the Jews called it 'Hanukka' and went to synagogue; the atheists went to parties and drank. People passing each other on the street would say 'Merry Christmas!' or 'Happy Hanukka!' or (to the atheists) 'Look out for the wall!'

Dave Barry

Now, instead of wishing everyone 'Merry Christmas', we are subjected to 'Season's Greetings', 'Happy Holidays' and 'Winter Festival' to name a few drippy, grey, generic tags dreamed up by the Take-Christ-out-of-Christmas crowd. I've actually heard the word 'holiday' used without any reference to what is being celebrated.

Mark Steyn

President George W. Bush is being criticized by Christian groups because his holiday cards don't have the word 'Christmas' in them. In response the President said, 'You try spelling it.'

Conan O'Brien

Memo to PC-potty Lambeth Council. Those bright twinkly things that go up in High Streets towards the end of every year are CHRISTMAS lights. They are not WINTER lights, CELEBRITY lights or any other bloody lights. I don't mind Diwali being called Diwali. Same with Ramadan and Yom Kippur. So why the hell should anyone object to the word Christmas?

Alan Edwards

Politically Correct Christmas

Oh how I wish that Charles Dickens was alive to attack such idiots [as Lambeth Council] with the eloquent mocking of his most satirical prose. Perhaps he would send his spirits to cure the misguided councillors of their tiptoeing fear of making any reference to the joy and good fellowship we find in Christmas. In any event, 'A Christmas Carol' should be made compulsory for them all so that they may know what Christmas is and Christmas can be and why it must be celebrated always.

John Mortimer

I like the name 'Winterval' instead of 'Christmas' because it sounds as if it lasts for three months and involves ice-skating in a tiny silver fox-fur dress while off your face on schnapps.

Caitlin Moran

For a performance in its 'winter program', a Wisconsin elementary school has changed the beloved Christmas carol 'Silent Night', calling the song 'Cold in the Night' and secularizing the lyrics. According to Liberty Counsel, a religious-liberty law firm representing a student's parent, kids who attend Ridgeway Elementary School in Dodgeville, Wis., will sing the following lyrics to the tune of 'Silent Night':

Cold in the night,
No one in sight,
Winter winds whirl and bite,
How I wish I were happy and warm,
Safe with my family out of the storm.

Worldnet daily, 7 December 2005

Politically Correct Christmas

Politically correct 'holiday' songs

- I'm Dreaming of a Many-Hued Winter Season
- Oh, Come All Ye Faithful, Agnostics and Atheists
- Frosty the Snowperson of an Indistinguishable Gender
- I Saw My Parent/Step Parent/Guardian/Caretaker Kissing Santa Claus
- Rudolph, the Reindeer with the Facial Appendage of a Different Colour
- Little Drummer Person
- Supreme Being of Your Choice Rest Ye Merry Gentlepeople
- We Wish You a Merry December

Mark Steyn

Rudolph the Nasally Empowered Reindeer.

James Finn Garner

They are now trying to politically correct up Christmas stories so that they don't offend nobody and that everybody everywhere can enjoy them. So this is a story that was formerly known as ''Twas the Night Before Christmas' ...

'Twas the night before a non-denominational winter
   holiday
And all through the house
Not a creature was stirring,
Not even a mouse.
The neutral gift sacks were hung by the chimney with care
In hopes that a non-specific holiday figure would be soon
   be there.
Children of every race, creed, and nationality
Were nestled snug in their beds
While visions of sugar-free plums
Danced in their heads.

Larry, Cable Guy

Politically Correct Christmas

... and all the Cratchits, including vertically challenged Tim, sat down to a delicious nut roast and toasted Mr Scrooge's recovery from post-traumatic stress disorder with a glass of sparkling mineral water.

James Finn Garner

What is so sad about all this religious censorship is that nearly every aspect of Christmas has a religious meaning. This means eventually the very celebration of Christ's birth will have to be destroyed. The New York public school system is doing just that by claiming that Christ's birth never happened!

Mark Steyn

Politically correct holiday greeting

Please accept without obligation, implied or implicit, our best wishes for an environmentally conscious, socially responsible, politically correct, low-stress, non-addictive, gender-neutral, celebration of the winter solstice holiday practised within the most enjoyable traditions of the religious persuasion of your choice, or secular practices of your choice, with respect for the religious/secular persuasions and/or traditions of others, or their choice not to practise religious or secular traditions at all. We wish you a fiscally successful, personally fulfilling and medically uncomplicated recognition of the onset of the generally accepted calendar year, but not without due respect for the calendars of choice of other cultures ... and without regard to the race, creed, colour, age, physical ability, religious faith, choice of computer platform, genetic secrets or sexual orientation of the wishee.

   (By accepting this greeting you are bound by these terms: this greeting is subject to further clarification or withdrawal. This greeting is freely transferable provided that no alteration shall be made to the original greeting and that the proprietary rights of

the wishor are acknowledged. This greeting implies no promise by
the wishor to actually implement any of the wishes.

This greeting may not be enforceable in certain jurisdictions
and/or the restrictions herein may not be binding upon certain
wishes in certain jurisdictions and is revocable at the sole
discretion of the wishor.)

Anon

Have yourselves a merry little seasonal day of enjoyment.

Mark Steyn

Have a Rama–Hana–Kwaz–mas.

Radio jingle, spoof PC greeting (Ramadan / Hanukkah / Kwanzaa)

Countdown to Christmas

Christmas is a funny old time. We spend one half of the year
planning for it and the other half paying for it.

Ilona Amos

There is no doubt … that being prepared is the secret of a
more harmonious Christmas. If Joseph had booked a room
in advance, Jesus would not have been born in a stable.

Jilly Cooper

If you really want to feel inadequate, flick through the
women's magazines for an update on the must–have
superior table decorations that you are meant to be
throwing together, the latest gift–wrapping techniques and
this year's intricate ways with turkey leftovers. I have just
spent three weeks languishing in hospital and believe me, I
have read them all – they might as well come under the
collective heading '101 ways to fail this Christmas'.

Miranda Ingram

Martha Stewart has already published her decorating calendar in the latest issue of her *Living* magazine: she's making Christmas cards on Dec. 2nd, tree skirts on the 4th and erecting a new greenhouse on the 8th. She strings the boxwood hedges with tiny lights on the 10th, hangs her handmade wreaths on the 14th and makes gift stockings on the 15th. The next day, she's making gingerbread tags for her presents. She goes to the Galapagos Islands three days after Christmas, then comes home and undecorates. 'January 9: Chip Christmas trees and use for mulch.'

Tamara Jones

I love Christmas, but, God, do I hate all the preparations leading up to it. And, God, do I want to kill all those selfless, super-organized forward-planners out there ... who start their Christmas shopping in the January sales, have everything wrapped, ribboned and labelled by mid-August and therefore now have time to do gay, festive things like bake gingerbread ornaments for the tree.

Christa d'Souza

Two days before C-day, there isn't anything to eat in the house apart from bananas and Vegemite; I have six more people to buy presents for and no time; everything needs vacuuming; and I can't stop yawning from my two-hour shopping trip to a surprisingly crowded Hamleys at 11.30 p.m.

India Knight

Christmas is a season of such infinite labour, as well as expense in the shopping and present-making line, that almost every woman I know is good for nothing in purse and person for a month afterwards, done up physically and broken down financially.

Fanny Kemble

Countdown to Christmas

There is one sentence guaranteed to bring gloom to the face of any mother with small fry: 'Christmas is for the children.' Because the corollary of Christmas being for the children is that Christmas is by mums. Tired mums. Broke mums. Mums who would like to believe that waving at someone from across the road is as good as sending them a card. Mums who love the idea of Christmas, but can't help seeing it as a huge month-long 'To Do' list.

Caitlin Moran

Perfectly managed Christmas correct in every detail is, like basted inside seams and letters answered by return, a sure sign of someone who hasn't enough to do.

Katharine Whitehorn

Jill Tweedie once wrote me a letter describing her Christmas: 'All we did was shop, cook, wash up; shop, cook, wash up …' Every household member believes that he or she is the only person who ever renews the loo-paper or the bin-liner, deals with coffee-grounds in the cafetiere, or empties the dishwasher (all too eagerly filled).

Valerie Grove

The best way to avoid fatigue, panic, or depression is to try to keep in mind that Christmas is intended as a celebration, not a contest.

Sandra Boynton

Sometimes I get in the bath with no water and just lie there. I've been known to have five 'baths' on Christmas Day.

Dawn French

We are not a family who take Christmas lightly: indeed, my mother has been known to call in lists of what we would each like some time during the summer holidays on the principle that the sooner she and Harrods get through with the shopping the sooner they can start planning for Easter.

Sheridan Morley

This year, can't we do Christmas ironically, put a Christmas stocking on Tracey Emin's bed, have Richard Rogers decorate the tree, get Germaine Greer to write a panto, with Tony Parsons as Buttons and Janet Street-Porter as Prince Charming?

A. A. Gill

Top Ten Things People Forget: batteries, cranberry sauce, camera film, hangover cures, enough milk, indigestion tablets, food for a vegetarian guest, spare light bulbs, tin foil and toilet rolls.

Rachael Bletchley

Instead of slaving in a hot kitchen making mince pies, brandy butter, Christmas cakes and fancy stuffing, why not buy them from a supermarket? Then you can spend your time enjoying yourself in the pub or at a party.

Lily Savage

Christmas Idyll: Widely held belief that if one somehow has a cottage in Suffolk, a deep-freeze, no television and temporary amnesia, they wouldn't be able to get at you.

Malcolm Burgess

I used to be taken to Christmas carols in Salisbury Cathedral. It always was cold in that shrine to austerity. The Anglican chants are drear: there is no joy in the ecclesiastical attempt at doo-wop ... I would never dream of taking my children to such a place. We'll do what we always do. I will have obtained, during the autumn, several hallucinogenic heads of the mushroom *amanita muscaria*. I have dried them and powdered them. We make cocktails of them. We get out of our heads.

Jonathan Meades

Even though Christmas can be a lot of work, we all know the bustle is worth the bother.

Lady Bird Johnson

Christmas Cards

Pre-holiday activities are the foreplay of Christmas. Naturally, Christmas cards are your first duty, and you *must* send one (with a personal, handwritten message) to every single person you ever met, no matter how briefly.

John Waters

Robins and reindeer, bunches of gilt bells, black cats, red-berried holly, Pickwickian coaches-and-four, candles, angels, fir trees … Each of us probably has in mind one ideal and absolute of the Christmas card, as received in childhood.

Elizabeth Bowen

My own ideal Christmas card (date around 1910) is this – I behold a cottage gable in deep-dusky silhouette against an expiring gleam of sunset, one window lit: smoke goes up from the chimney. To this, a woodman returning, footprint by footprint, across the foreground snow: all around stretch white wastes, the bare trees are dark. How it glows and glows through that one small window – core of the world, magnet to man, the home!

Elizabeth Bowen

Shop crowded with people, who seemed to take up the cards rather roughly, and after a hurried glance at them, throw them down again. I remarked to one of the young persons serving, that carelessness appeared to be a disease with some purchasers. The observation was scarcely out of my mouth, when my thick coat-sleeve caught against a large pile of expensive cards in boxes one on top of the other, and threw them down. The manager came forward, looking very much annoyed …

George Grossmith, The Diary of a Nobody

Sorry, no more Christmas cards left – only religious ones.

London shop assistant

[In the House of Commons] I sat right through the Brandt report debate without getting called to speak … I did the Christmas card list on my lap, periodically making objectionable interruptions.

Alan Clark, MP

Sending Christmas cards too early is not only ineffective but can be humiliating for the sender. It reveals one's position, discloses the size and quality of card, exposing oneself to the possibility of a devastating counter-attack. On the other hand, a very late Christmas card runs the risk of negating the recipient's ability to respond, and reduces one's total card count.

William Connor

Christmas cards are just junk mail from people you know.

Patricia Marx

The literary agent Pat Kavanagh has a robust attitude: picks up cards from doormat, opens them, tears them up and puts them straight in the bin.

Valerie Groves

Christmas Cards

Michael Winner, the nation's favourite shrinking violet, considers himself 'the master of the Christmas card'…The Winner missive of 2005 … is a photograph of a smiling Winner, standing beside the Queen … Last year, Winner's card featured a photograph of him as a baby, while previous years have included Winner as a fairy; Winner having knocked down Santa Claus; and Winner having shot Santa, with one leg placed upon him in triumph.

Ed Caesar

– More Christmas cards? Are they genuine or are they more of those you've written to yourself?
– I regard it as a service to those people who may have misplaced my address. I'm sure they'd like to think they sent me a card.

Richard and Hyacinth Bucket, Keeping Up Appearances

I've even heard that some people save this year's cards to display again next year, anyway. All I'm saying is that's what I've heard.

Deborah Ross

Rats. Nobody sent me a Christmas card today. I almost wish there weren't a holiday season. I know nobody likes me. Why do we have to have a holiday season to emphasize it?

Charlie Brown, A Charlie Brown Christmas

Much hilarity in the Private Office at an e-mail from the top floor. It advises them that 'The Queen's Christmas card has arrived.' We are cordially invited to visit the mantelpiece to admire it.

Robin Cook, Foreign Secretary

The Queen has sent about 37,500 Christmas cards during her reign.

Eighty Things About Queen Elizabeth II, 2006

Christmas Cards

Some people get very competitive when it comes to Christmas cards ... I would never try to bump up my own Christmas cards by displaying the ones that say, inside, 'Free garlic bread with all orders until December 31' as those really shouldn't count.

Deborah Ross

There is also a place for very small and/or very cheap Christmas cards. They imply bad taste, poverty or disrespect to the recipient, and will guarantee deletion from their Christmas card list. These are particularly effective for terminating pointless long-term Christmas card exchanges with people like the Fanshaws you met in Torremolinos ... and can't even remember what they look like any more – or was it Benidorm?

William Connor

Do you want to feel insecure? Count the number of Christmas cards you sent out, and then count those you received.

Milton Berle

What are you supposed to do with other people's family-portrait Christmas cards, welcome as a box of Matchmakers? We make merry by drinking a lot and then uproariously deciding who is trying hardest to look successful and harmonious, and who therefore had the worst year and most arguments.

Gillian Ferguson

Much has been written about the Prime Minister's Madonna-and-child study with Cherie and Leo, which comes with a scrawled 'Tony and Cherie', clearly written by just one hand. To be honest, isn't sending a photograph of yourself at Christmas the height of egomania? Couldn't Cherie and Tony just have given us little Leo in a swaddling

Christmas Cards

Timberland sweatshirt and stayed out of the limelight? I suspect the reason they didn't is that Christmas cards have become status symbols. It's not how many you get, but who they come from.

Janet Street-Porter

Our Christmas greeting cards are mostly from businesses wishing us heart-felt pre-printed bulk-mailed holiday wishes like:

'Tis now a time for Peace on Earth
And Joy for all Mankind
So let us know if we can help you
Unclog your sewer line.

Dave Barry

I'd just opened a card from Carol and Sam. I have no idea who they are either, but Carol, Sammy, you have the ugliest children on God's earth. The thing on the left is a real monster, and they're getting pride of place just above the coal scuttle.

A. A. Gill

I was glad to get a letter instead of a Christmas card. A Christmas card is a rather innutritious thing.

Oscar W. Firkins

You know those Christmas cards that play a tune when you open them? Well, I don't know if you've ever taken one apart but there's a little button attached to a wire. I once knew a TV producer who, as a dare, wrapped one of these up in smoked salmon and swallowed it. For half an hour after, if you went up to his stomach I swear you could hear 'Good King Wenceslas'.

Phillip Schofield

The Christmas card perfectly sums up our age —
impersonal, garish, emotionally threadbare and egotistical.
An age when what things look like is more important than
what they actually mean.

Janet Street-Porter

Then there are the round robins, which summarize the past
year with news of offspring who are all, it seems, adept on
the violin, adore singing madrigals and win places at
Oxbridge. (A prize one last year even said: 'Jamie is now at
Edinburgh, having turned down Cambridge …') My
husband threatens to respond with fearlessly frank robins
detailing our children's shaming misdemeanours.

Valerie Grove

Maggie is walking by herself. Lisa got straight As. And Bart
… well, we love Bart.

Marge Simpson, writing her round-robin letter, The Simpsons

God, how they all hated those newsletters. Iris should have
made *The New York Times'* best-seller list for fiction. Who
else had kids who were toilet trained at seven months, guest
conductor for the Atlanta Symphony at six, and sent thank-
you notes in French? Their family picture on the letter
made the Osmond family look depressed.

Erma Bombeck

In our family we sometimes play the Christmas card game.
All Christmas cards received are dealt out to players, who
then take it in turns to nominate a category, such as the
ugliest Christmas card, the one with the most cherubs, the
snowiest, or whatever. Each player then offers his best for
the category and all argue about who should win.

Charles Moore

O Christmas Tree

As well might we dance without music, or attempt to write a poem without rhythm, as to keep Christmas without a Christmas tree.

The Weekly Press

The Christmas tree was proof that Narnia, fairies and hobgoblins and fauns truly did exist. For the tree miraculously appeared overnight and it shed such light and a divine perfume. Being small, I could sit under it all evening with the glass baubles dancing in my face.

Toyah Willcox

In the window of a large house in Morningside ... stood a tree decorated tastefully and ungaudily with simple white bows. On closer inspection the bows proved to be ingeniously constructed from those perforated strips of computer paper, torn off, looped and stapled. A decoration guaranteed to satisfy ... stern Scots Nonconformists.

Valerie Grove

Fir: tree which keeps its leaves all year round except during Christmas.

Mike Barfield

Frost and snow. Ted and I nearly lost our fingers pulling snow-frozen ivy off the trees to decorate the cottage. The car broke down, we had great difficulty in collecting the Christmas trees from Jackson's farm and Ted got into quite a suicidal mood. But I said that it is always a good sign when things go wrong before the night.

Barbara Castle

I saw a guy driving down Hollywood Boulevard with a tree on his front bumper and I said, 'Getting ready for Christmas?' He said, 'No, teaching the wife how to drive!'

Bob Hope

The major varieties of Christmas tree are: Pine, Spruce, Douglas Fir, Walnut, Fake, Balsa, and Douglas Firbanks Jr. Before you buy a tree, you should always have Dad pick it up and bang it hard on the ground a couple of times.

Dave Barry

Did you know that Christmas trees are edible? I don't recommend it, nor do I have a suitable recipe but, apparently, the needles are a good source of vitamin C.

Sandi Toksvig

Even living alone as I do, I am considering buying a small Christmas tree and putting it in front of my television set to block out the millionth screenings of *The Magnificent Seven* and *The Sound of Music* plus the awful Terry Wogan et al.

Jeffrey Bernard

When I was around nine, I cut a flat tree out of green wrapping paper and pinned it to my bedroom wall, next to my poster of Marc Bolan, and wet bed chart. I covered all three in glitter.

Tracey Emin

You can tell a lot about a man by the way he handles three things: a rainy day, lost luggage, and tangled Christmas tree lights.

H. Jackson Brown, Jr

O Christmas Tree

When decorating the tree, always use strings of cheap lights manufactured in Third World nations that only recently found out about electricity and have no words in their language for 'fire code'.

Dave Barry

My mother and father had a festive time decorating the Christmas tree. I watched them hanging the baubles with a heavy heart. I am reading *Crime and Punishment*.

Adrian Mole

But Mother gave the tree life with stories about nearly every ornament: one was a long-ago gift from her sister, another had come from Germany with our grandmother, others had been made by Conny and me in kindergarten … With ornaments of such a rich heritage, how could our tree be anything but magnificent? Yes, Mother knew how to make the night – and the season – special.

Barbara Bradlyn Morris

Tree-trimming parties get the halls decked and the boughs filled with baubles while providing a chance to see friends. If you are very brave or have far too many friends, you can do it as an afternoon eggnog party. If you haven't already got one, borrow or rent a large silver punch bowl, fill it with that rich and potent punch, set out platters of tea sandwiches and Christmas cookies and hope the tree gets trimmed … The tree should be up and the lights wound 'round before the guests arrive.

Susan Dooley

Then some friends came round for a tree-decorating party. I had envisaged this occasion as a glowy, WASPy sort of thing, with people in woolly jumpers standing around, clinking glasses of eggnog with each other. But it wasn't like that at all. It was just a bunch of grumpy Jews ordering takeaway

Thai food and arguing about the rights and wrongs of a war
with Iraq, while the children stamped up and down on the
fairy lights and got bauble splinters in their hands.

Zoë Heller

– Where do you keep your knighthood medal?
– Well, at Christmas I hang it on the tree.

Conan O'Brien and Sir Ian McKellen

I have been looking on, this evening, at a merry company
of children assembled round that pretty German toy, a
Christmas tree. The tree was planted in the middle of a
great round table, and towered high above their heads. It
was brilliantly lighted by a multitude of little tapers; and
everywhere sparkled and glittered with bright objects.

Charles Dickens

For our Christmases at home Dixie insisted on a big tree. It
had to be tall enough to reach from floor to ceiling.
Sometimes it was touch and go whether she'd lop off a few
feet of tree or call for the wreckers to cut a hole in the roof.

Bing Crosby

Never worry about the size of your Christmas tree. In the
eyes of children, they are all thirty feet tall.

Larry Wilde

White and gold-only trees, co-ordinated table spreads and
prettily dressed cadeaux are for consenting adults, not
family Christmases. A friend with two toddlers still tortures
herself trying to maintain the colour co-ordinated
decorations she was so proud of when a childless bride.
Your children will bring home bags of art-class decorations,
and these must have pride of place.

Miranda Ingram

O Christmas Tree

Oh the wonder of this Christmas day ... The tree touched the ceiling and was heavy with tinsel and snow and candles – but who can describe a Christmas tree? The scent of pine, the cheery mystery of the packages below, the charm of the very top star, the flickering little candles ...

Anaïs Nin

We have a 10ft-high fake tree because Neil is allergic to real fir trees. We are devoted to our Christmas fairy, who must be at least 55 years old. She has lost a leg but swathed in fresh tinsel and with a light on her wand she looks absolutely fine.

Christine Hamilton

The best Christmas trees come very close to exceeding nature.

Andy Rooney

When I'm looking at a well-decorated Christmas tree, no amount of adverse experience can convince me that people are anything but good.

Andy Rooney

Going into the drawing room, [Mark] was astonished to see that during the night the brightly coloured glass balls hanging from the branches of the tree had been added to by long looping garlands of French letters. Luckily, with Jane's and my help we managed to remove them all in time for the Reverend and Mrs Worsley, who were popping in for their annual pre-Christmas lunch drink.

Annabel Goldsmith, describing the antics of her father,
the 8th Marquis of Londonderry

Remember, if Christmas isn't found in your heart, you won't find it under the tree.

Charlotte Carpenter

Deck the Halls! Christmas Decorations

Man is born free but is everywhere in paper chains.

Jilly Cooper

For many of us who grew up in the 1950s, '60s and '70s, the season officially began when Mom brought the big boxes out from storage, packed with all the shiny totems of the season: round Shiny Brite tree ornaments of multicoloured, gossamer-thin glass; garlands of silver tinsel that looked like something Liberace might wear around the house; scale-model country churches whose steeples lit up when you plugged them in; and enough injection-moulded Santas, reindeer, snowmen and flock-watching shepherds to fill Christmas Island – or the island of Taiwan, whence many of them came.

Jeff Turrentine

Tinsel is really snakes' mirrors.

Steven Wright

Genitalia? Is that the silver stuff you drape over the branches?

Anita, Dinner Ladies

My young daughter disposed of my £2 coins in the dustbin because they had no chocolate inside.

Chris Jeffrey

This morning, I saw on the High Street a Santa Claus statue about the size of a seven-year-old. He says 'Ho ho ho!' and he sings a song. Instantly, I thought I'd buy it. He's now in the kitchen next to the statue of Jesus and I'm waiting for the grandchildren to see it. That'll become a ritual every year, when this blinking Santa will come out and go 'Ho ho ho!'

Beryl Bainbridge

– Is your house on fire, Clark?
– No, Aunt Bethany, those are the Christmas lights.

Aunt Bethany and Clark Griswold, Christmas Vacation

We have many homeowners who cross the fine line, in terms of illumination, between 'tasteful holiday yard display' and 'municipal airport'. You know the houses I mean: the ones with a Frosty the Snowman the size of Godzilla; the ones with so many lights in the trees that you need an umbrella to avoid being struck by the falling bodies of electrocuted squirrels.

Dave Barry

Roseanne, your Christmas decorations outside were appalling. The wise men are supposed to be adoring the baby Jesus, not leering at Mrs Claus.

Bev, Roseanne

– Dad, what are you doing with that wreath?
– I'm gonna hang it on the front door like I always do.
– But it's *plastic*!
– Of course it's plastic! Do you think a real one would have lasted since 1967?

Frasier and Martin Crane, Frasier

The white icicle lights came first, delicate and twinkly on her garden apartment balcony. They were so pretty, she bought more. The icicles turned into manic sheets of brilliance, like after an avalanche. Then came the colours: blues, pinks, purples, greens. Then the computerized LED lights. Then the fibre-optic Christmas tree with the stuffed tarantula on top. Then the glowing pink palm tree. Llori

Stein couldn't stop. Stein's Christmas balcony disaster – her words – is now so ugly, in fact, that the Falls Church deck appears on the Web site www.uglychristmaslights.com, which documents people who 'have no sense of decency in how they choose to celebrate'.

Brigid Schulte

It's not hard to create an ugly display. All you have to do is get carried away. I look like Christmas regurgitated all over my balcony. There are very few displays that look that good. And if they look that good, it's kinda boring. When I see Christmas lights, I want to laugh.

Llori Stein

With the bling-driven determination of P. Diddy on a trolley dash round Asprey's, the desire to light up the outsides of houses with enormous effigies and huge lettering, ramming home the high-wattage, unequivocal merriness of Christmas, has spread like viral flu through a geriatric ward.

Judy Rumbold

Do you expect me to illuminate the street simply by my presence?

Princess Michael of Kent having difficulties turning on Christmas lights in Jermyn Street, London, 2000

Why is it that when snooty department stores put their Christmas decorations out just after the 4th of July it's 'elegant foresight', but when I leave my Christmas lights up until April, my neighbours think I'm just tacky?

Alisa Meadows

Do you do this with Christmas tree lights? You have a string of them and one bulb is dead, and you flick the bulb with your finger to get it to light up? Same thing they do with George Bush before a debate.

Jay Leno

Deck the Halls!

It's official – retired builder and local councillor Danny Meikle, 56, puts on Britain's biggest home-made festive lights extravaganza with his annual shrine to Yuletide. It has taken him six weeks to decorate his home in Coalburn, Lanarkshire, with one million Christmas lights, musical trees and Santa's grotto – resulting in a display so bright it's used by pilots as a turning point.

Daily Express, 2003

Celebrities love the season of goodwill to all men. No need to put up Christmas lights – they just crank up the power on their electric fence until it's white hot.

David Letterman

My best Christmas was a few years ago, when there was a power cut from Christmas Eve morning until Boxing Day afternoon. We had no lights, no heating and ate smoked salmon sandwiches round the fire. It was such fun with all the candles. My nephews adored it.

Christine Hamilton

Real bachelors do not feel the urge to put up Christmas decorations. Except sometimes when they get very drunk and sentimental on Christmas Eve. If this happens to you, paint your behind red and green and press it against the front window.

P. J. O'Rourke

Christmas wouldn't be Christmas without the Blue Peter Advent-Candle Holder.

Malcolm Burgess

Each of us creates our own special times at Christmas. We find our special ornaments, hang the mistletoe, and place the star as we have done before. There is a comforting certainty in the sameness – a promise of continuity.

Lady Bird Johnson

Perhaps the best Yuletide decoration is being wreathed in smiles.

Anon

Let It Snow! Winter Weather

I have often thought, says Sir Roger, it happens very well that Christmas should fall out in the Middle of Winter.

Joseph Addison

In this country there are only two seasons, winter and winter.

Shelagh Delaney

I prefer winter and fall, when you feel the bone structure of the landscape – the loneliness of it – the dead feeling of winter. Something waits beneath it – the whole story doesn't show.

Andrew Wyeth

Winter. The landscape has turned from a painting to an engraving.

Thomas Hardy

Winter could drop down out of a clear sky, sharp as an icicle, and, without a sound, pierce your heart.

Jessamyn West

What a lovely thing a bit of fine, sharp, crystallized broken snow is, held up against the blue sky catching the sun – talk of diamonds!

John Ruskin

Let it Snow!

Signs it will be a hard winter: both of London's gritting lorries go in for a service. The central heating boiler blows up.

Anon

There seems to be so much more winter than we need this year.

Kathleen Norris

Up in the morning's no for me,
Up in the morning early!
When a' the hills are cover'd wi' snaw,
I'm sure it's winter fairly!

Robert Burns

Let no man boast himself that he has got through the perils of winter till at least the 7th of May.

Anthony Trollope

Then English winter – ending in July to recommence in August.

Lord Byron

Winter in Madison Square was tamed like a polar bear led on a leash by a beautiful lady.

Willa Cather

Winter is the time for comfort, for good food and warmth, for the touch of a friendly hand and for a talk beside the fire: it is time for home.

Edith Sitwell

On winter days the classrooms smelt of snow-dampened wool ... Since our britches and socks and the girls' lisle stockings frequently had snow on them, only partially stamped off in the cloakroom, the classrooms took on the not unpleasant odour of moist wool drying.

Robert MacNeil, Wordstruck

Let it Snow!

The weather so far is fine and Yuleish with quite a lot of
snow. I dread a thaw and a slushy Christmas but perhaps the
Almighty will be amiable; after all, it is a celebration of his
own boy's birthday.

Noël Coward

Fine old Christmas, with the snowy hair and ruddy face,
had done his duty that year in the noblest fashion, and had
set off his rich gifts of warmth and colour with all the
heightening contrast of frost and snow … But old
Christmas smiled as he laid this cruel-seeming spell on the
outdoor world, for he meant to light up home with new
brightness, to deepen all the richness of indoor colour, and
give a keener edge of delight to the warm fragrance of
food; he meant to prepare a sweet imprisonment that
would strengthen the primitive fellowship of kindred, and
make the sunshine of familiar human faces as welcome as
the hidden day-star.

George Eliot, The Mill on the Floss

This has been a foggy morning and forenoon, snowing a
little now and then, and disagreeably cold … At about
twelve there is a faint glow of sunlight, like the gleaming
reflection from a not highly polished copper kettle.

Nathaniel Hawthorne

That night in bed, the sheets were hard and slippery,
unfriendly as ice. Carefully, by an act of will, Bernard made
a warm place in the bed exactly the same shape as his body,
thin and hunched under the covers. He extended it
gradually, inch by inch, sending his toes gently into the cold
until he was at last straight and comfortable.

Leslie Norris

In winter the temperature falls well below the legal minimum.

Douglas Adams

Let it Snow!

One Christmas – years agone now, years – I went the
rounds wi' the Weatherbury quire. 'Twas a hard frosty night,
and the keys of all the clarinets froze, so that 'twas like
drawing a cork every time a key was opened.

Thomas Hardy, Under the Greenwood Tree

So cold, so bitterly cold, and both of us so stiff, that we were
medieval, and spent the day in bed.

Sylvia Townsend Warner

It was so bitterly cold that the wine as well as the water
freezes in the glasses at the King's table.

Charlotte-Elisabeth, Duchesse d'Orléans, 1695

It is freezing fit to split a stone.

Marie de Rabutin-Chantal

I was so cold when I was in England, I almost got married.

Shelley Winters

We were a very poor family. We were so poor we couldn't
afford central heating. At Christmas, I and my whole family
would sit round a candle and if it was really cold we used to
light it.

Brian Conley

It was so cold that when I tried to blow out the candle, the
flame was frozen, so I had to snap it off.

Anon

It's so cold that cows are giving cream by the scoop.

Anon

… my ink froze in the glass on the Standish – yesterday two
bottles of water, which I keep in my study, froze and burst
the bottles, one of which I gently knocked the glass of the

bottle from and the ice in the bottle, neck and all; one mass of ice, just the shape of the bottle.

John Baker, 1776

My beard was frozen on my mackintosh ... There was a large christening party from Llwyn Gwilym. The baby was baptized in ice which was broken and swimming about in the font.

Reverend Francis Kilvert

The frost severer than ever in the night as it even froze the Chamber Pots under the Beds.

Reverend James Woodforde

But it is immensely cold – everything frozen solid – milk, mustard, everything.

D. H. Lawrence

The cold increases, the snow is getting deep, and I hear the Thames is frozen over very nearly, which has not happened since 1814.

Queen Victoria, 19 January 1882

Today is the coldest day of all; frost feathers, flowers, ferns all over the windows, giving a dim clouded light inside; my pen frozen, so that I could not write with it or fill it. Then broadest sunlight pouring on to me in bed, warm, melting the frost flowers so that a steam goes up, waving, wreathing its shadow across this page as I write. I have a lot to do.

Denton Welch, 1947

Cold! If the thermometer had been an inch longer we'd have all frozen to death!

Mark Twain

Let it Snow!

It's so cold in New York that the Statue of Liberty is holding the torch *under* her dress.

David Letterman

Last night, it was so cold, the flashers in New York were only describing themselves.

Johnny Carson

They had to jump start Al Gore it was so cold.

Jay Leno

It was so cold in New York yesterday, a pregnant woman went into labour when her ice broke.

Joan Rivers

It's really cold in New York. Lingerie departments are now selling thermal thongs.

Joan Rivers

Cold hands, warm heart.

English proverb

In Minnesota it's so cold some nights you have to wear two condoms.

Bruce Lansky

You know you're in Alaska when ...
- You own more than four pairs of gloves.
- You find −60°C a mite chilly.
- The boot of your car doubles as a deep freeze.
- You attend a formal event in your best clothes, your finest jewels and your ski boots.
- You can play road hockey on ice skates.
- Shovelling the driveway constitutes a great upper body workout.

Let it Snow!

- When it warms up to −35°F and you go out in your shirtsleeves to wash your car.
- You think sexy lingerie is fleece socks and a flannel nightie.
- You don't know anyone who doesn't own a four-wheeler.
- You are holidaying in Hawaii when a beautiful woman in a bikini walks by and you think, 'Boy, I'd sure like to see her in a snowmobile suit.'
- Instead of plugging in your freezer you just move it to the front porch.

Anon

The coldest winter I ever spent was a summer in San Francisco.

Mark Twain

I love Christmas in Miami. Oh, sure, it's not like Christmas up north. We don't have Jack Frost nipping at our nose; we have Harvey Heat Rash nipping at our underwear regions. And we never look outside on Christmas morning to discover that the landscape has been magically transformed by a blanket of white, unless a cocaine plane has crashed on our lawn.

Dave Barry

One way to cope is to escape abroad – ideally to a remote, tropical island, which takes courage and cash. A couple of years ago we went to Disneyland, Paris but all we did was fraternize with other escapees who, like us, felt slightly guilty. It didn't really make Christmas go away or become more spiritual. We simply had to have Christmas lunch with 2,000 people in a hall. It was like taking part in a Mormon mass wedding.

Helen Lederer

Let it Snow!

I had Christmas in LA ten years ago; the sun was shining and it wasn't fun. I need cold, snow, grim London and repeats of *The Two Ronnies* and Bruce Forsyth.

Paul McKenna

To enjoy Christmas in LA, you have to accept the fact that you're going to be listening to Nat King Cole crooning 'Chestnuts Roasting on an Open Fire' next to an infinity pool surrounded by palm trees.

Sarah Standing

Christmas is emphatically not a festival that ought to be celebrated in shorts.

Zoë Heller (in southern California)

I have always felt it deeply unpatriotic to go to a warm climate for Christmas. It's not a real Christmas unless your breath hangs in the cold air and the sun sets in time for afternoon tea.

Robin Cook

Green Christmas, white Easter.

German proverb

> Bless my eyes,
> Here he lies,
> In a sad pickle,
> Kill'd by an icicle.

Epitaph, St Michael and All Angels' Church, Bampton, Devon

Kicking horsedung – how it echoes to the merry walker on a frosty morning.

S. T. Coleridge

The room was cold and through the opened window came the fresh smell of snow like the moist nose of an animal resting on the ledge and breathing into the room.

Ben Hecht

Let it Snow!

I did Christmas presents, finishing the last card for the USA, and in the afternoon, out of a dark sky, small white pellets of snow rattled on the house. I ran down the drive for pleasure, eating them.

Sylvia Townsend Warner

Never eat yellow snow.

Anon

The first fall of snow is not only an event but it is a magical event. You go to bed in one kind of a world and wake up to find yourself in another quite different, and if this is not enchantment, then where is it to be found?

J. B. Priestley

Snow makes you silly. We threw snowballs, fell over, laughed, pushed each other and generally behaved like children. That's the point of snow.

A. A. Gill

For those who find hand-packing their own ammo for a snowball fight to be too much trouble, the latest edition of the Martha Stewart catalogue features the Snoballer. The bright red plastic tool, which looks like two crisscrossed ladles that open and close like fireplace tongs, is designed to scoop and shape snow into uniform fist-size snowballs. Doesn't that take the fun out of it? Not for Martha Stewart. 'I was impressed with the perfectly round forms ... but was especially happy with the fact that my hands didn't get cold and wet after hours of playing outdoors ... The snowballs didn't hurt. They exploded on contact, unlike hand-packed ones.'

Dany Levy

How full of creative genius is the air in which these are generated! I should hardly admire them more if real stars fell and lodged on my coat.

Henry David Thoreau

Let it Snow!

Are the angels sawing timber in heaven? See how they lift their planks in the flour-loft and shake the dust down on us; and they wear cloaks of frosty silver trimmed with coldest quicksilver.

Anon

The snowflake is a delicate puzzle of geometrical beauty, this tabletop from fairyland, like a spider's web frosted as it floated through the air.

Wilson A. Bentley

Every man's woodlot was a miracle of surprise to him, and for those who could not go so far there were the trees in the street and the weeds in the yard ... you might say that the scene differed from the ordinary one as frosted cake differs from plain bread. In some moods you might suspect that it was the work of enchantment. Some magician had put your village into a crucible and crystallized it thus.

Henry Thoreau

Around all and beyond all, was the snow, almost exactly resembling the snow that fell in English films on top of people like Alistair Sim and Margaret Rutherford.

Clive James on first arriving in England from Australia

In January 1494 a great deal of snow fell in Florence and Piero de' Medici ... wanted a statue of snow made in the middle of the courtyard. He remembered Michelangelo, sent for him and had him make the statue.

Ascanio Condivi, assistant to Michelangelo, 1553

The snow hid all the grass, and all signs of vegetation ... We played at cards – sate up late. The moon shone upon the water below Silver-How, and above it hung, combining with Silver-How on one side, a bowl-shaped moon, the curve downwards; the white fields, glittering roof of

Let it Snow!

Thomas Ashburner's house, the dark yew tree, the white fields gay and beautiful. William lay with his curtains open that he might see it.

Dorothy Wordsworth

We stopped to look at the stone seat at the top of the hill. There was a white cushion upon it, round at the edge like a cushion, and the rock behind looked soft as velvet, of a vivid green, and so tempting! The snow too looked as soft as a down cushion.

Dorothy Wordsworth

We came back powdered with snow, all three of us – the little bull-dog, the Flemish sheepdog and I … Snow had got into the folds of our coats, I had white epaulettes, an impalpable sugar was melting in the wrinkles of Poucette's blunt muzzle, and the Flemish sheepdog sparkled all over … sheepdog – 'steaming like a footbath … listens to the whispering of the snow against the shut blinds'.

Colette

The snow was thick, and in the afternoon the sky cleared, and the landscape looked as if it had gone to heaven.

Sylvia Townsend Warner

A deep snow upon the ground … We walked through the wood into the Coombe to fetch some eggs. The sun shone bright and clear. A deep stillness in the thickest part of the wood, undisturbed except by the occasional dropping of the snow from the holly boughs; no other sound but that of the water, and the slender notes of a redbreast, which sang at intervals on the outskirts of the southern side of the wood.

Dorothy Wordsworth

Snow is falling outside my window, and indoors all around me half a hundred garden catalogues are in bloom.

Katharine S. White

Let it Snow!

It is not until you see sheep against snow that you realize that they are, in fact, grey.

Miles Kington

Brain scan: Inside the head of a snowman

I'm dreaming of a white Christmas … I'm dreaming of a white Christmas … I'm dreaming of a white Christmas … I'm dreaming of a white Christmas … I'm dreaming of a white Christmas … I'm dreaming of a white Christmas … I'm dreaming of a white Christmas … I'm dreaming of a white Christmas …

The Times

The wisdom of a single snowflake outweighs the wisdom of a million meteorologists.

Sir Francis Bacon

Snowflakes are one of nature's most fragile things, but just look what they can do when they stick together.

Vesta M. Kelly

They say that every snowflake is different. If that were true, how could the world go on? How could we ever get up off our knees? How could we ever recover from the wonder of it?

Jeanette Winterson

There is salvation in snow.

Elizabeth Weber

I think the whole world should be covered with snow; it would be so much cleaner.

Norma Shearer, Idiot's Delight

I'm dreaming of a white Christmas. This song could only be sung in southern California around a swimming pool.

Let it Snow!

Here, at the first hint of snow British Rail runs to a standstill, the roads become impassable, and even the pavements are a danger as the salt destroys your shoes.

Derek Jarman

A lot of people like snow. I find it an unnecessary freezing of water.

Carl Reiner

I am told that the Inuit have some 60 words for snow ... I have 17 words for snow – none of them usable in public.

Arthur Black

I don't want to find fault, but I wonder if God ever considered having snow fall up?

Robert Orben

A man shovels snow for the same reason he climbs a mountain – because it's there.

Nathan Nielsen

A good snow machine will cost $2,000 and last four to five years. With dogs, you've got regenerative powers. Snow machines don't have pups.

Lou Schultz, trainer of Alaskan Huskies

Snow Blower for Sale. $230 or nearest offer. Only used on snowy days.

Classified ad in the Minnesota Echo

Most of [Iceland's taxes] seem to go on clearing snow, which is a bit like paying God Danegeld. A task that makes Sisyphus look like he's got a hobby.

A. A. Gill

Let it Snow!

We sometimes wonder why the City Government tilts so vigorously at the snow. The first flake has hardly fluttered down when every infernal machine in town is rushing to do battle ... Is snow such poisonous stuff? Our own feeling is that it is something to be honoured and preserved – and we would like to see all citizens provided with little tinkling bells so that they would make merry sounds as they plodded about their business, in high rubber boots.

E. B. White

How do the men who drive the snowplough get to work in the morning?

Steven Wright

On Friday morning I was amazed to see, along with dozens of other passengers at Northwick Park station, my train approaching the platform preceded by two men walking slowly along the line scraping snow off the rails with spades. Have we reached the ultimate in British technology?

Rita Keyes

One service the railways offer that still runs like clockwork is the cancellation of Christmas trains.

Keith Waterhouse

It was the Wrong Kind of Snow.

Terry Worrall explaining disruption on British Rail, 1991

My advice to anyone contemplating travelling in snow: stay home.

Samuel Johnson

The Eskimos have 52 names for snow because it was important for them: there ought to be as many for love.

Margaret Atwood

Let it Snow!

There's more to Inuit culture than famously having 50 words for snow, a fact that has never impressed me anyway, because, after all, the British have a thousand words for rain.

Victor Lewis-Smith

Albeit snow is very beautiful when falling, its loveliness passes away very shortly afterward. The grand poetical result is merely chilblains and slush.

Mark Twain

Snow is all right while it's snowing; it is like inebriation because it is very pleasing when it is coming, but very unpleasing when it is going.

Ogden Nash

Snow on 25 December is now about as rare as a tip from the old Scrooge himself.

Geoffrey Lean

What it does here at Christmas is rain. We should make this a meteorological virtue. Let us have a British Santa in cheery yellow oilskins and sou'wester, ho-ho-hoing through the drizzle in a dory tugged by six big cod. Let fake raindrops twinkle down our shop windows from autumn on, let our cards show robins on floating logs and coaches in flying spray … Sing 'I'm Dreaming of a Wet Christmas', Cliff, and let's be done with it.

Alan Coren

Unless we make Christmas an occasion to share our blessings, all the snow in Alaska won't make it 'white'.

Bing Crosby

Santa Claus is Coming to Town

Heap on more wood!
The wind is chill,
But let it whistle as it will,
We'll keep our Christmas merry still.

Sir Walter Scott

Surely everyone is aware of the divine pleasures which
attend a wintry fireside: candles at four o'clock, warm
hearth rugs, tea, a fair tea-maker, shutters closed, curtains
flowing in ample draperies to the floor, whilst the wind and
rain are raging audibly without.

Thomas De Quincey

There's snow on the fields,
And cold in the cottage,
While I sit in the chimney nook
Supping hot pottage.

Christina Rossetti

May you have warm woods on a cold evening, a full moon
on a dark night, and the road downhill all the way to your
door.

Irish blessing

Santa Claus is Coming to Town

Christmas is a national holiday for the greedy. What is
Father Christmas if not the patron saint of greed? For in
decreeing that only good children will get presents, he
reduces the simple joy of behaving well to a premeditated
strategy for material gain. And good for him.

Giles Conran

Santa Claus is Coming to Town

When I was a kid, I hated Christmas because I believed in Santa Claus. Unfortunately, so did my parents, so I never got any presents.

Charlie Viracola

I remember when I was about six, a friend of mine said, 'There's no Father Christmas, you know.' And I said, 'Yes, there is, because last year he brought me lots of presents.' And my friend said, 'No, Father Christmas doesn't exist ... it's your dad.' And I didn't know whether to be really upset or really excited – the fact that *my* dad, every Christmas, got into a sleigh and went round the whole world delivering presents to all the boys and girls.

Rory McGrath

My worst Christmas was the discovery that Santa Claus was none other than my father. Every year I made a special effort to stay awake and see Father Christmas. I'd left out the cake and glass of milk for him as usual. My parents used to have a few whiskies and talk while they waited for me to fall asleep. This year, though, I heard my father come in and say: 'I'll eat the cake but I'm not drinking the bloody milk.' It was quite a shock at the time ...

Sara Parkin

I tried and succeeded in catching Father Christmas when I was seven. I laid a quite intricate trap involving bells, a low bench and a poker in my bedroom. I awoke at midnight to the sound of cursing and the sight of my dad spreadeagled on the ground with a broken ankle. I got no stocking for another three years ...

Dom Joly

My husband is so cheap. On Christmas Eve he fires one shot and tells the kids Santa committed suicide.

Phyllis Diller

Santa Claus is Coming to Town

Like everyone in his right mind, I feared Santa Claus.

Annie Dilliard

Santa is a genuinely sinister figure. Think about it: a single, old man watches everything little children do, because he wants to know which are the naughty ones. People have been hounded out of town by anti-paedophile mobs for far less.

Julian Baggini

What example of family bonding does Santa Claus set, deserting his wife and kids on Christmas Eve for an all-night house-crawl?

Francis Wheen

There are anthropologists who claim that Santa's irrepressible hilarity and ability to fly are the result of midwinter revellers ingesting large quantities of magic mushrooms. Ho, ho, ho! Indeed!

Will Self

I played Santa Claus many times, and if you don't believe it, check out the divorce settlements awarded my wives.

Groucho Marx

Santa Claus comes under many names: Kris Kringle, Saint Nicholas, MasterCard ...

Phyllis Diller

My kids seem to regard me as a life-long Father Christmas.

Harry Burton

I was brought up a communist. It was Lenin who came down our chimney at Christmas.

Alexei Sayle

Santa Claus is the leading symbol of the hagiography of US mercantilism.

Fidel Castro

Santa Claus is Coming to Town

It has been calculated that Santa's team of nine reindeer
would emit methane with a global warming impact
equivalent to more than 40,600 tonnes of greenhouse gases
on the 122-million-mile Christmas Eve dash to deliver
presents around the world. That would make his marathon
sleigh ride almost as environmentally damaging as an
aircraft ... The methane calculations were made by Liberal
Democrat transport spokesman Tom Brake. He said the best
Christmas present for the environment would be if Santa
took the bus ... although he admitted the annual trip might
take a bit longer than usual.

Raymond Hainey

You can't fool me. There ain't no sanity claus.

Chico Marx

[*Saying his bedtime prayers*] Dear Santa, if you bring lots of
good stuff, I promise not to do anything between now and
when I wake up.

Bart Simpson

I stopped believing in Santa Claus when I was six. Mother
took me to see him in a department store and he asked for
my autograph.

Shirley Temple

Not believe in Santa Claus! You might as well not believe in
fairies! You might as well get your papa to hire men to
watch all the chimneys on Christmas Eve to catch Santa
Claus, but even if they did not see Santa Claus coming
down, what would that prove? Nobody sees Santa Claus,
but that is no sign that there is no Santa Claus. The most
real things in the world are those that neither children nor
men can see.

Francis P. Church

Santa Claus is Coming to Town

Our home is a place in which Santa still lives and reigns supreme at Christmas time. I have never been one for political correctness and have no wish of being a rebel without a Claus.

Tony Deyal

There've been over four hundred documented sightings of Santa Claus. Scientifically documented. And it's on the Internet, so you know it's true.

Manny, Monk

You know you're getting old when Santa starts looking younger.

Robert Paul

The three ages of man: he believes in Santa Claus; he doesn't believe in Santa Claus; he is Santa Claus.

Donald Guthrie

Yes, Virginia, there is a Santa Claus. He exists as certainly as love and generosity and devotion exist, and you know that they abound and give to your life its highest beauty and joy.

Francis P. Church, editorial in the New York Sun, 1897, in response to a letter from eight-year-old Virginia O'Hanlon asking if there is a Santa Claus

Remember, hang on to your youth as long as you can. The minute you stop believing in Santa Claus, you get socks and underwear for gifts.

Pat Williams

Now I know there is a Santa Claus.

Edmund Gwenn, on winning Best Supporting Oscar for his role as Kris Kringle in Miracle on 34th Street, 1947

Was there ever a wider and more loving conspiracy than that which keeps the venerable figure of Santa Claus from slipping away, with all the other old-time myths, into the forsaken wonderland of the past?

Hamilton Wright Mabie

As Father Christmas on our Rotary float recently, I asked one little girl if she had written to tell me what she wanted for Christmas. She replied: 'No, my computer has crashed.'

Tony Walker

Santa is having a tough time this year. Last year he deducted eight billion for gifts, and the Inland Revenue wants an itemized list.

Milton Berle

Our local department store had two Santas – one for regular kids and one for kids who wanted ten toys or less.

Milton Berle

According to research … British homes will be adding to Santa's fat belly this year by leaving him 18 million mince pies, 9 million glasses of sherry and at least a million chocolate biscuits, giving him two million times as many calories as he needs and five million times the recommended number of units of alcohol.

William Hartston

I understand there is some gossip among these citizens because they claim a Santa Claus with such a breath on him as our Santa Claus has is a little out of line.

Damon Runyon

Another crisis! I've heard that Santa's drunk and he's holding a painting by a French 18th century pastoral artist and a piece of paper out of a cracker. Oh no! He's blotto in the grotto with a Watteau and a motto.

I'm Sorry I Haven't a Clue radio show

Santa Claus is Coming to Town

Drunken Santas on a rampage in New Zealand, armed German robbers in Santa disguises, a British St Nick wanted for flashing, and a Swedish vandal in a Santa outfit are giving the big man in red a bad name this year.

Reuters news agency, 2005

Five Irritating Habits of Santa Claus. 1) Wearing boots indoors. 2) Saying 'Ho ho ho'. 3) Letting his beard go skew-whiff. 4) Barging unannounced into private parties. 5) Being overweight.

Craig Brown

Come July, I look at my razor, and put it away again. I don't shave then until Boxing Day so I have a real white beard. Children always notice and whisper, 'He must be the real one.' I love doing it – I have more fun than the kids.

Dan Jones, 'Birmingham's Best-Loved Father Christmas'

He's going to have to lose twenty even to get Santa Claus work come Yuletide.

Peter De Vries

Santa is even-tempered. Santa does not hit children over the head who kick him. Santa uses the term 'folks' rather than 'Mommy' and 'Daddy' because of all the broken homes. Santa does not have a three-martini lunch. Santa does not borrow money from store employees. Santa wears a good deodorant.

Jenny Zink, memo to employees of Western Temporary Services, world's largest supplier of Santa Clauses

Smell nice. Don't ask about mummies and daddies because they have usually run off with milkmen. Don't say 'Yo-ho-ho'. It frightens the children. Practise weightlifting. Don't mention chimneys because a lot of children haven't got one. Don't promise anything. And don't wear glasses. If

asked, 'Where's Rudolph?' always say he's miles away.
Otherwise, they will all be out in the car park looking for
him and causing a public nuisance.

Sue Overbury, advice to trainee Santas

Only last month, one in the north of England was sacked
for giving a toy gun to a child with the words, 'Take that
and shoot Margaret Thatcher.'

Stephen Pile, 1985

It is no wonder that the experience of visiting Santa at
Harrods, the luxury department store with a full-fledged
grotto, delivers all the cheer of a rugby scrum in the mud.
People line up outside in the cold before opening hours and
then sprint through the doors the moment they open.
Parents dash up the escalators, thwacking elbows, body
checking their competitors and dragging their children
behind them, only to line up again for hours inside the store.

Lizette Alvarez

'Santa Land': queues. Garish lights. Irritating music. Horrid
logos everywhere … Cubicles of identical Santas lined up
like hookers in a Soho peep joint (complete with filthy
sofas). Rip-off photo (child terrified, Santa checking
watch). Six-second ride with a 20-minute queue (the
mythical snow slide). Bored, disgruntled staff. All this for the
bargain price of £25 an adult, £20 a child and a £15 flat
parking fee … But quite the most extraordinary thing
about the whole sorry show was that the children I was
with (six of them, aged one to six) absolutely loved it.

Sarah Vine

They err who think Santa Claus comes down through the
chimney; he really enters through the heart.

Mrs Paul M. Ell

67

Santa Claus is Coming to Town

Santa's message is simply this: magical possibilities exist in the universe.

Sam Rosenberg

I still even believe in Santa Claus. I'm sure the children must have told me that he isn't real. But I have never believed them.

Nancy Reagan

Maybe, when you come to think about it, grown-ups need Father Christmas far more than children do.

Anon

The great thing is not to believe in Santa Claus; it is to be Santa Claus.

Pat Boone

Living with Elton is like living with Santa Claus. Show an interest in anything and it will just appear.

David Furnish, partner of Sir Elton John

Santa is very jolly because he knows where all the bad girls live.

Dennis Miller

Hey, Santa, how much for your list of naughty girls?

Anon

Santa comes but once a year ... too bad!

Mae West

Does My Bum Look Big in This Suit? How to Become a Department Store Santa

OK, so it's seasonal work, the money's not great, and you'll be fired on Christmas Eve, but if you become a department store Santa for once in your life you're *not* just another fat guy – you're THE MOST FAMOUS PERSON ON THE PLANET. Forget Dr Who, Mickey Mouse and the Teletubbies, the memory of meeting you will be something kids will treasure for the rest of their lives.

Job Description

It has to be the only job where the older you get, the more weight you put on, and the more facial hair you grow, the more successful you'll be. You'll also need a twinkle in your eye, a taste for mince pies, and a high threshold of pain when it comes to piped versions of 'Jingle Bells'. And don't forget to brush up on current trends in toys, music and movies. Kids will suss you immediately if you don't know your Xbox from your X-men. Any convictions for snorting fairy dust or interfering with little drummer boys are best kept under your Santa hat. And keep schtum about your appearance on the Jerry Springer Show called, 'I Slept with Rudolph to Make Dasher Jealous'.

So ferocious is the competition for the department store Santa gig that candidates are now required to sit a written test to qualify for a BSc (Bachelor of Santa Clausing). But the good news is: an elf working undercover has got hold of the test paper so steal a march on the competition with this sneak preview …

Does My Bum Look Big in This Suit?

1. Santa's first question when a small boy sits on his lap is
   a. Have you ever seen a reindeer fly?
   b. Have you ever seen an elf high?
   c. Have you ever seen a fat guy naked?

2. To calm a nervous child, Santa offers to let him
   a. ride his skidoo
   b. tickle him under his beard
   c. hold his sack

3. Ho Ho __
   a. Yo!
   b. D'oh!
   c. Blow!

4. Santa enters a house through the
   a. chimney
   b. looking glass
   c. cat flap

5. Santa's favourite Christmas Eve snack is
   a. reindeer burger
   b. elf fricassee
   c. a six pack of Bud and a family pack of Doritos

6. I saw Mommy _____ Santa Claus underneath the
   mistletoe last night
   a. kissing
   b. punching
   c. shagging

7. Which of these is not the name of a reindeer?
   a. Dasher
   b. Prancer
   c. Lap Dancer

8. _____ roasting on an open fire
   a. Tiny Tim
   b. Frosty the Snowman
   c. Tony Blair

9. What religion is Santa?
   a. Amish
   b. Kabbalah
   c. Scientology

10. Pick the adjective that does not apply to Santa
    a. jolly
    b. merry
    c. wasted

Holly Robinson

Christmas Shopping

I'm a rabid sucker for Christmas. In July I'm already worrying that there are only 146 shopping days left. I'm always the Little Drummer Boy for Halloween.

John Waters

Once again, we come to the Holiday Season, a deeply religious time that each of us observes, in his own way, by going to the mall of his choice.

Dave Barry

Another day, another million dollars.

Richard Donat, store manager, Marshall Field & Co., Chicago

Angels we have heard on high
Telling us to go and buy!

Tom Lehrer

Christmas Shopping

Even before Christmas has said 'Hello' it's saying 'Buy, buy.'

Robert Paul

The annual Winter Shoppers Festival – formerly known as
Christmas – begins some time after the last Easter egg
leaves the shelves and just before the first firework is sold.

Brian Swanson

From a commercial point of view, if Christmas did not exist
it would be necessary to invent it.

Katharine Whitehorn

Life requires reason, selfishness, capitalism; that is what
Christmas should celebrate – and really, underneath all the
pretence, that is what it does celebrate. It is time to take the
Christ out of Christmas, and turn the holiday into a
guiltlessly egoistic, pro-reason, this-worldly, commercial
celebration.

Leonard Peikoff

The best aspect of Christmas is the aspect usually decried
by the mystics: the fact that Christmas has been
commercialized.... It stimulates an enormous outpouring of
ingenuity in the creation of products devoted to a single
purpose: to give men pleasure. And the street decorations
put up by department stores and other institutions – the
Christmas trees, the winking lights, the glittering colours –
provide the city with a spectacular display, which only
'commercial greed' could afford to give us. One would have
to be terribly depressed to resist the wonderful gaiety of
that spectacle.

Ayn Rand

Since Christmas is a big feast for all corporate brands, we
might as well reposition it as that. Enjoy Christmas for what
it really is: swap all the religion for what really matters –

material possessions. With that in mind, pick any of the following stars and worship them. Merry Christmas (from: PlayStation, Apple, Coca-Cola, Gucci, Barbie, Microsoft, Calvin Klein, Fisher-Price, Mattel, Nokia, Disney, H&M, McDonald's, Nike, Mercedes, Panasonic, Ericsson, Motorola, Sony, Hewlett-Packard, Ford, Gillette, MGM, Compaq, Honda, Budweiser, Pepsi, Oracle, Samsung, Holiday Inn, Penguin group, Morgan Stanley, Dell, Toyota, Nintendo, Kodak, Gap, HSBC, Kellogg's, BMW, Canon, Heinz, Volkswagen, Ikea, Champion, Harley-Davidson, Louis Vuitton, MTV, L'Oreal, Xerox, KFC, Orange, Accenture, Avon, Philips, Nestlé, Warner Bros, Chanel, Kraft, Selfridges, Yahoo!, Hoover, Bacardi, Adidas, Rolex, Omega, Tiffany, Duracell, IBM, Hermes, Jack Daniels, Levi's, Hertz, Hennessy, Shell, Smirnoff, Prada, Moet & Chandon, Nissan, Heineken, Nivea, Electrolux, Starbucks, Polo Ralph Lauren, FedEx, Visa, Topshop, Guinness, Boots, British Airways, Paul Smith, Cartier, Audi, Diesel, Bally, Burton, Lacoste, Harrods, Boss, Fila, Seiko, Hallmark, Kronenbourg, Lancome, Minolta, Puma, Red Bull, SAAB, Volvo, Siemens, Whirlpool …

'Mother' Advertising Agency, rebranding Christmas

As to economics, we might not be 'less in debt' without Christmas purchases, because … over one quarter of the year's retail business is transacted [during the Christmas season] in everything from department stores to grocery stores. Without this holiday volume, year-round prices could be higher, and fewer jobs might be available.

Helen Dunn Frame

Who says doing Christmas shopping early avoids the crush? Last year, I did mine a full twelve months in advance, and the shops were just as busy as ever.

Gavin McKernan

Christmas Shopping

You may be a redneck if … you go Christmas shopping for your mom, sister and girlfriend and you need buy only one gift.

Jeff Foxworthy

Once again we found ourselves enmeshed in the Holiday Season, that very special time of year when we join with our loved ones in sharing centuries–old traditions such as trying to find a parking space at the mall. We traditionally do this in our family by driving around the parking lot until we see a shopper emerge from the mall, then we follow her, in very much the same spirit as the Three Wise Men, who 2,000 years ago followed a star, week after week, until it led them to a parking space.

Dave Barry

If you want to restore your faith in humanity, think about Christmas. If you want to destroy it again, think about Christmas shopping.

Reno Goodale

Christmas is like going to war. Going down to Oxford Street is hanging over me like going over the top.

Bridget Jones, Bridget Jones's Diary

This is such a dangerous time of year with all this goodwill about and everybody in such a temper because of Christmas shopping. As I remarked long ago to the ambient air of Whitleys Ltd:

> The time draws near the birth of Christ
> When everything is overpriced.

Sylvia Townsend Warner

– I don't know which present to buy first.
–You should always buy the first gift for the person you love the best.
– But, Doris, *I've* got everything.

Bing Crosby and Doris Day

Outside, our new Ann Summers sex shop was drumming up trade by sending into the traffic-jammed streets a gigantic truck hauling a vast hoarding, perhaps 15 feet high, plastered with pictures of young women wearing almost nothing, the whole topped with the legend 'COME all ye faithful', which even I thought a shade tasteless.

Simon Hoggart

I was in a department store and I saw a weird-looking gadget. I asked the young saleslady what it was. She answered, 'It doesn't do anything. It's just a Christmas gift.'

Milton Berle

Christmas is no time for practical presents … Words and phrases that can be taken as green flags, indicating that you are on the right track, include 'preposterous', 'packed in natural feathers' and 'Made in Botswana'.

Mike McClintock

Never give a loved one a gift that suggests they need improvement.

H. Jackson Brown, Jr

Christmas, yes! Either people tell me what they want and I can't get it, or they don't tell me what they want and I can't think of anything. I think it was Peter Warlock who said, 'It is a time of year I dislike more and more as I get older.' Amen to that.

Philip Larkin

Christmas Shopping

The saying, 'It's the thought that counts' was coined as an emotional Band-Aid by someone who left all of her shopping until nine o'clock Christmas Eve … If it's really the thought that counts, then why don't we ever tell people what we were thinking when we were scrambling to buy them their last-minute panic-gift? 'It was under twenty dollars and I hardly ever see him that much anyway.'

Ellen DeGeneres

The first rule in buying Christmas presents is to select something shiny. If the chosen object is of leather, the leather must look as if it had been well greased; if of silver, it must gleam with the light that never was on sea or land. This is because the wariest person will often mistake shininess for expensiveness.

P. G. Wodehouse

The Increasingly Desperate Guy Shopper is trying to find something for that Special Someone in his life, who has made it clear that this year she'd like something a little more personal than what he got her last year, which was a trailer hitch.

Dave Barry

Avoid purchasing your Christmas presents at the last minute. Gifts from the 24-hour garage are rarely appreciated as much as those from Harrods or even Woolworth's, and unwrapping a litre of two-stroke oil or a Cornish pasty on Christmas morning will test the blindest love.

Jeff Green

Christmas is the season when people run out of money before they run out of friends.

Larry Wilde

Spending a lot of money, especially the bank's, on presents
doesn't make you a good person or buy affection ... Think
back to your own favourite Christmas memories, and if
they are not of when times were hard, presents few, simple,
inexpensive or home-made, but the emotions genuine and
heartfelt, then I'll eat my paper hat.

Fordyce Maxwell

Christmas gift suggestions: To your enemy, forgiveness. To
an opponent, tolerance. To a friend, your heart. To a
customer, service. To all, charity. To every child, a good
example. To yourself, respect.

Oren Arnold

In the context of Christmas and the Holy Year of
Redemption, I was able to meet with the person that you
all know by name, Ali Agca, who in the year 1981 on the
13th of May made an attempt on my life. But Providence
took things in its own hands, in what I would call an
extraordinary way, so that today ... I was able to meet my
assailant and repeat to him the pardon I gave him
immediately.

Pope John Paul II

My True Love Gave to Me: Christmas Presents

I love Christmas. I receive a lot of wonderful presents I can't
wait to exchange.

Henny Youngman

My True Love Gave to Me

– Bart, you will *not* be getting a tattoo for Christmas.
– Yeah, if you want one, you'll have to pay for it out of your own allowance.

Marge and Homer Simpson, The Simpsons

I was glad to hear of a friend who listened to his children's extravagant demands until he could stand it no more. 'This is ridiculous,' he cried. 'In my day, we thought ourselves lucky if we got a stocking with just an apple and an orange inside.' 'Bloody hell,' muttered his eldest kid. 'A computer and a mobile phone, and that's just in the stocking …'

John Walsh

Every year, one of my children wants a game for Christmas. It is always one for which the demand exceeds the supply by about 355,000. Every kid in town has it on his list … The game is touted on television, beginning in June, with the approach that if it is not under your tree on Christmas Day you are an unfit parent and your child will grow up to rob convenience stores wearing pantyhose over his face.

Erma Bombeck

I know someone, who knows someone, who knows an elf. And if any of you children acts up, so help me I will call Santa and tell him you want socks for Christmas!

Lynette Scavo, Desperate Housewives

How are we manipulated into buying toys we cannot afford and are interesting for a matter of minutes? Several reasons: For one, parents are basically insecure and have to buy affection, and second, we are cursed with short memories. We refuse to stop and reflect on toys past that have been discarded … the ping-pong table. It was a big table that held books, coats, dirty laundry, lunch bags, stuff that had to go to the cleaner, and stacks of old newspapers. You couldn't see the TV over it, and it eventually went to the garage, where it warped.

Erma Bombeck

My True Love Gave to Me

William Morris said never have anything in your home unless you believe it to be beautiful or know it to be useful – it's a good rule. Christmas quickly turns our homes into temples of well-intended, but totally unwanted, clutter, and we all know the sadness of mustering a smile when we receive something we're going to bang straight into Oxfam on New Year's Eve.

Alan Young

I'm giving everyone framed underwear for Christmas.

Andy Warhol

In December 1948 a Washington radio station telephoned various ambassadors in the capital, asking them what they would like for Christmas. The unedited replies were recorded and broadcast in a special programme the following week. 'Peace throughout the world,' proclaimed the French ambassador. 'Freedom for all the people enslaved in imperialism,' demanded the Russian ambassador. 'Well, it's very kind of you to ask,' came the voice of Sir Oliver Franks, the British ambassador. 'I'd quite like a box of crystallized fruits.'

Geoffrey Moorhouse

I spend Christmas with my Irish parents, brother and nephew at the family home in London and I still feel a sense of wonderment getting up on Christmas morning and seeing everyone's faces when they open their gifts. I spend a lot of time choosing a present that will reflect what is unique about the person. Most people buy presents they want themselves, but I listen carefully all year and when I hear a clue to what someone wants, I store it in my head.

Paul McKenna

My True Love Gave to Me

An informal survey shows that what most people want for Christmas is two more weeks to prepare for it.

Bob Stanley

– Well, Rose, it's a beautiful blouse.
– I hope you like it. Dorothy said you would like something crotchless.

Blanche and Rose, The Golden Girls

So much, indeed, is there to be said for and against any view about giving presents, that it is safer not to think about it, but to buy your presents first, and afterwards to consider what, if anything, you will do with them. After all, if you decide in the end not to give them to anyone, you can always keep them.

Rose Macaulay

Even as a child, I was embarrassed by Christmas. First of all, it's my birthday. My mother gave me two shillings to buy a present for my father, and my father gave me two shillings to buy a present for my mother, and they both thanked me! I felt a terrible fool. You get presents you're never going to be able to use, and you have to thank people for them, and they thank you for presents they're never going to be able to use.

Quentin Crisp

This year I have discovered a novel way of hiding my family's Christmas presents. I simply stack them on the stairs, where they become immediately invisible – just like all the other junk that lurks there.

Clare Desai

My True Love Gave to Me

Three phrases fill the air at Christmas time: 'Peace on Earth', 'Goodwill to all Men' and 'Batteries Not Included'.

Tony Deyal

There are a lot of things money can't buy. None of them are on my Christmas list.

Joan Rivers

I bought presents of humbug and fudge, which I think are representative of what you can expect from the House of Commons.

Ann Widdecombe, visiting a centre for the homeless

Hollywood – climate and religious diversity notwithstanding – is a Christmas kind of place. And if one doesn't send out hundreds of Christmas cards (sample message: 'May the Joy of the Season Warm You and Your Family. A donation in your name has been made to an Important-Sounding Charity'), send gift baskets of tiny, inedible muffins, and in general behave as if one day's generosity can somehow mitigate 364 days of cruelty and selfishness; well, then, just how does one expect to succeed in this town?

Rob Long, Set Up, Joke, Set Up, Joke

I bought my son an indestructible toy. Yesterday he left it in the driveway. It broke my car.

Milton Berle

My father gave me a bat for Christmas. The first time I tried to play with it, it flew away.

Rodney Dangerfield

Christmas is the time of year kids get toys their fathers can play with.

Milton Berle

My True Love Gave to Me

Last Christmas, I gave my kid a BB gun. He gave me a sweatshirt with a bullseye on the back.

Rodney Dangerfield

My parents, my whole life, combined my birthday with Christmas, and you know how frustrating that is for a child – especially as I was born in July.

Rita Rudner

I remember the Christmas when I was six years old. I asked for a set of felt-tip pens – the big set with all the colours from lemon yellow to mahogany. When I discovered my present all wrapped up on Christmas Eve, I felt it … yes, yes, it's the felt-tips! Imagine my disappointment the following day … pan pipes.

Harry Hill

I've never enjoyed the holidays. There was the time in eighth grade when my mother wouldn't let me open my presents until I had finished reading *Sense and Sensibility*. So I sat scowling at the book for three days until finally, on December 28, she relented. I haven't read a page of Jane Austen since.

Alec Kuczynski

There are six evacuated children in our house. My wife and I hate them so much that we have decided to *take away* something from them for Christmas!

James Agate, diary entry, 22 December 1939

Your presents to us made a Christmas inside a Christmas. I was in great need of the seaweed emulsion. It doesn't say specifically what it is for.

Sylvia Townsend Warner

The nice thing about a gift of money is that it's so easily exchangeable.

Arnold Glasgow

My True Love Gave to Me

The Wise Men's gifts are … undeniably Christmassy. They're the kind of stuff that today you might still give to near-strangers, neighbours, in-laws, distant cousins and your child's teacher, or buy as emergency presents, in case a spare relative drops by. Incense sticks, perfumed candles, pot pourri, Terry's All Gold chocolates, costume jewellery, gold-leaf picture frames …

John Walsh

Ah, pot pourri! Where would we be without it? It says so much. It says, I don't know you very well, but am obliged because of circumstances to give you something. It's the kind of thing sister-in-laws give each other.

Marian Keyes

Christmas is the time of year when virtually anything can be fobbed off as a fancy gift, provided that it's nestling in a basket on a bed of straw and packed in cellophane. Whether containing small phials of body lotion (each containing enough to cover approximately half a thigh), miniature jars of tartan-lidded service station marmalade or cute toy kittens with bows on, the straw to gift ratio is generally 90:1.

Catherine Barnes

– We're going to have a baby. That's my Christmas present to you.
– All I needed was a tie.

Woody Allen

Men are amused by almost any idiot thing … But you should never buy them clothes. Men believe they already have all the clothes they will ever need, and new ones make them nervous. For example, your average man has 84 ties, but he wears, at most, only three of them.

Dave Barry

My True Love Gave to Me

Unsure what to buy the men in your life? – Gift packs are a waste of money. For every item that he'll actually use – moisturizer, shaving cream – there will be at least two more – superdream eyebrow glaze, inter-toe soothing balm, etc. – that clog up his bathroom shelves until the day he dies.

James Delingpole

The best gift I've ever had was my husband giving up smoking – it was the only thing I asked for that year.

Hayley Cooper

Christmas worries me. My wife buys me gifts I can't afford.

Jack Lewis

There is always somebody that you're afraid not to give a Christmas present to.

Anon

I made a terrible mistake last Christmas. My wife made me swear that I wouldn't give her a fancy gift. And I didn't.

Milton Berle

Ever since Eve gave Adam the apple, there has been a misunderstanding between the sexes about gifts.

Nan Robertson

The last time I attempted to buy lingerie for my other half I failed miserably. Cup sizes? That's what they offer at Starbucks, isn't it? After an hour of lurching around in the undies department, I did the manly thing and opted for vouchers.

Rob Singh

Rule number one: never buy a woman anything with a plug attached. Rule number two: never buy a man anything with a head hole. Willy holes are fine.

A. A. Gill

My True Love Gave to Me

Women are never what they seem to be. There is the woman you see, and there is the woman who is hidden. Buy the gift for the woman who is hidden.

Erma Bombeck

A good gift must be either hopelessly extravagant, something you could never afford or justify. Or it should be something delightfully odd that you would never have thought of yourself. Or something purely pleasurable. The common thread is surprise and delight.

Stephen Bayley

In our house, it's almost magical when, every Christmas Eve, my wife Plum pulls out a beautifully wrapped present and asks me to write on the label 'To Plum with love from Ray', not forgetting to add those three fond kisses. Presents are supposed to be a surprise, and I'm always as surprised to see what I've bought her as much as what she's bought me.

Ray Connolly

The one thing women don't want to find in their stockings Christmas morning is their husband.

Joan Rivers

I gave my wife a gift certificate for Christmas. She ran out to exchange it for a bigger size.

Milton Berle

If you want to give a man something practical, consider tyres. More than once, I would have gladly traded all the gifts I got for a new set of tyres.

Dave Barry

My True Love Gave to Me

Last Christmas, my son bought me a set of mongrammed handkerchiefs with the letter 'D' on them. I said, 'Why do they have a "D" on them?' He said, 'They were in the sale.'

Rick Wakeman

There's a gift to inadvertently offend that not-so-special person in your life in virtually every store at Christmas. Unlike genuine bad taste novelty gifts such as chocolate reindeer poo or giant underpants, these offerings are well meant but sadly misguided … Hand-painted teapots 'for one' look delightful but they are a poisoned chalice (for one). This gift will confirm the lonely singleton's fear of yet another 365 days with only a packet of Hob Nobs for company.

Catherine Barnes

I love Michael Jackson. He's my best friend. I buy him a handkerchief for Christmas each year. I don't know what to buy him this year. He has no nose. No nose. What do you buy a man with no nose?

Joan Rivers

The best Christmas present I ever got was two cows. Because it was Christmas and they are both female, I called them Mary and Josephine.

Billie Piper

A hug is the perfect gift – one size fits all, and nobody minds if you exchange it.

Ivern Ball

Charlie Watts sends me the best Christmas presents. Bronze Age swords. Medieval daggers. There's a lot of thought behind that. Mick Jagger will send me an orchid … something like that. Keith Richards sends me the same thing every year – a candle.

Bill Wyman

My True Love Gave to Me

—You know, Chandler, you being here is the best gift I
could ask for Christmas.
— Aww. Thanks Pheebs.
— OK, now where's my *real* present?

Phoebe Buffay and Chandler Bing, Friends

A nose job is the best Christmas present ever because you'll
have it for ever. It's not like some sweater you don't like and
have to take back to the store.

Helena Rasin

The worst Christmas present I was ever given was a 'Grow
Your Own Loofah Kit' from my sister.

Sean Lock

The worst Christmas present I ever received was a shoe-
cleaning set. Romance never really went a lot further after
that deep token of devotion.

Keith Elliot

… the boyfriend who bought me a pair of bathroom scales
from Comet shortly after he'd told me I had fat arms.

Lisa Armstrong

I know that I have given some ghastly gifts. I cringe to think
of the year when everyone received 'Character Candle
Snuffers', made out of glazed pottery, all of which had cutesy
names. The only proper place for such things is a dustbin.

Ann Treneman

With her regular gifts of shoe-trees Aunty Kath had
hitherto held the record for boring Christmas presents, but
Bill shows he is no slouch in this department either when
he presents me with the history of some agricultural
college in New South Wales (second volume only). 'You
did history, Alan. This should interest you.'

Alan Bennett

My True Love Gave to Me

My worst present? Gardening tools I received when I was living in a second-floor flat.

John O'Byrne

The worst Christmas present I ever received was a Bugs Bunny record player, received at the age of ten. While this may sound delightful, I didn't own any records. What's more, it would play only seven-inch discs – which simply didn't exist in Hong Kong, where I spent my formative years. Attempts to use it as a potter's wheel resulted in a small fire and a lot of molten plastic.

Mark Rapeli

My worst Christmas was when I was just married and staying with my new mother-in-law. She was very frugal and used old wrapping paper for her presents. Mine was covered in elegant black writing which said: 'To darling Leo with all my love'. It had been from his first wife.

Jilly Cooper

My friend's mother-in-law gave her the worst present ever: a used soap-on-a-rope – embedded with pubic hair.

Arabella Weir

My worst Christmas present was from my mother-in-law. She bought me a portable urine collector with female adaptor (a potty, basically) for use on our long family journeys.

Philippa Jones

Several years ago, I was in a job that I was about to be sacked from. Right before I left, we were asked to participate in a Christmas pot-luck party to which we would bring anonymous presents to be exchanged with other presents … My contribution was a roll of toilet paper, a vodka bottle half-filled with water, a voodoo doll and a gift certificate to an adult bookstore. At least it made my parting with the company sweet.

Andrew Gallagher

The strangest present I ever received, though it wasn't an unpleasant one, was a buffalo skin complete with the buffalo's head. When we put it down in the hall our daughters wouldn't walk over it because they thought it implied cruelty to animals. It was given by some people in the US who shared my views about currencies, and lived in buffalo country. It is now in the loft.

William Rees-Mogg

My present to all members of the Government would be a humble pie.

Nicholas Russell

In this house the Chancellor is known as 'suck a lemon Brown'. Therefore I would like to send him, for Christmas, a sack of lemon slices so that every time I see him with that prissy, prim, disapproving look on his face I will know that he really is sucking lemons.

David Fowler

I've organized a Secret Santa – a week beforehand the kids will draw family names out of a hat to arrange at random who buys a present for who, with a set price limit, to cut down on the pressure of having to buy something for everyone. It's great fun, too. That's what Christmas is about, after all.

Jamie Oliver

Christmas won't be Christmas without any presents.

Louisa May Alcott, Little Women

My True Love Gave to Me

Dear Santa Claus, How have you been? Did you have a nice summer? How is your wife? I have been extra good this year, so I have a long list of presents that I want. Please note the size and colour of each item, and send as many as possible. If it seems too complicated, make it easy on yourself: just send money. How about tens and twenties?

Sally Brown, A Charlie Brown Christmas

You never have to figure out what to get for children, because they will tell you exactly what they want. They spend months and months researching these kinds of things by watching Saturday-morning cartoon-show advertisements.

Dave Barry

Our children await Christmas presents like politicians getting election results; there's the Uncle Fred precinct and the Aunt Ruth district still to come in.

Marceline Cox

No matter how many Christmas presents you give your child, there's always that terrible moment, when he's opened the very last one. That's when he expects you to say, 'Oh, yes, I almost forgot,' and take him out and show him the pony.

Mignon McLaughlin

Nothing's as mean as giving a little child something useful for Christmas.

Kin Hubbard

As a kid, sometimes my Christmas present was an orange. We were poor and fruit was a once-a-year thing. To this day, that's why I still love the smell of oranges.

Dolly Parton

My True Love Gave to Me

One Christmas things were so bad in our house that I asked Santa for a yo-yo and all I got was a piece of string. My father told me it was a yo.

Brendan O'Carroll

I was so poor growing up, if I hadn't been born a boy I'd have had nothing to play with on Christmas Day.

Rodney Dangerfield

A truly appreciative child will break, lose, spoil or fondle to death any really successful gift within a matter of minutes.

Russell Lynes

All those presents, ingenious devices for taking money off you for things other people don't want in return for things you don't want yourself, in fact you often don't just not want them, you find them positively offensive. So that's the kind of book/tie/bottle of booze/gadget they think I'd appreciate, you mutter aggrievedly.

Kingsley Amis

Fewer and fewer people in Britain are having children … Perhaps we should concentrate on our pets. An advertising feature in the Telegraph Magazine recently offered a made-to-measure tartan kilt for dogs, at £99.95 … If one cancelled all other presents and celebrations, I feel this might be a good way of marking the Birth of Our Saviour in present circumstances. At least the Pekingese would wag their little tails.

Auberon Waugh

A lot of Americans got high-definition TVs for Christmas, which means a lot of celebrities will be seeing more of their plastic surgeons this year.

Joan Rivers

My True Love Gave to Me

There are many people – happy people, it usually appears – whose thoughts at Christmas always turn to books. The notion of a Christmas tree with no books under it is repugnant and unnatural to them.

Robertson Davies

My first copies of *Treasure Island* and *Huckleberry Finn* still have some blue-spruce needles scattered in the pages. They smell of Christmas still.

Charlton Heston

I'm already signing books for husbands to give their wives at Christmas. When I ask if I should put 'Darling Dorothy' or 'To my sweetest Elizabeth' or what exactly, they always say, 'No. To She Who Must Be Obeyed.'

John Mortimer

Who wants to be given a novel? Fiction as a gift is like a hat or a bikini: only the wearer can possibly know whether it suits.

Valerie Grove

The most loathsome of all this year's crass Yuletide innovations is surely the 'ethical Christmas gift'. Instead of the DVD or handsome pair of socks you'd been hoping to receive, an ecologically crazed friend posts you a charity card informing you that 'the money I would have spent on your present has been used to buy six chickens for an African farmer' or 'a camel for a Bedouin tribesperson', and you're supposed to look pleased that he's given you precisely nothing, while he basks in a nauseating glow of self-satisfied eleemosynary.

Victor Lewis-Smith

And on Christmas morning, after the gifts have been opened, what are the kids doing? Playing with boxes and snapping the air pockets of plastic packing material.

Erma Bombeck

Remember that the more a toy costs, the more likely kids will want to play with the box it came in.

H. Jackson Brown, Jr

Friends of mine … were awoken on Christmas morning last year by howls of protest from their two sons. 'These stockings are crap!' the ten-year-old yelled. 'We're going to sue Santa Claus.'

Francis Wheen

The price of Christmas toys is outrageous – a hundred dollars, two hundred dollars for video games for the youngsters. I remember a Christmas years ago when my son was a kid. I bought him a tank. It was about a hundred dollars, a lot of money in those days. It was the kind of tank you could actually get inside and ride in. He played in the box it came in. It taught me a very valuable lesson. Next year he got a box. And I got a hundred dollars' worth of scotch.

Johnny Carson

One of the most glorious messes in the world is the mess created in the living room on Christmas Day. Don't clean it up too quickly.

Andy Rooney

Last year for Christmas, I got a humidifier and a dehumidifier. I thought I'd put them in the same room and let them fight it out.

Steven Wright

My True Love Gave to Me

We cannot give in the true Christmas spirit if we do not give to those who cannot afford to give anything in return.

Clare Booth Luce

Simple gifts such as a compliment, a note, a telephone call or a simple act of kindness – these are the truest forms of giving because they come from the heart – they are literally a portion of the giver.

David Dunn

The commercialism always makes me nauseous. Long ago I did a 'deal' with the kids: no presents, but I'll take them to the sales afterwards.

Edwina Currie, Diaries

A puppy isn't just for Christmas. If you're lucky, there should be enough left over for Boxing Day dinner as well.

Anon

–Your first Christmas as a new mum – what present would you like?
–You can't wrap pelvic floors, can you?

Interviewer and Fay Ripley

If any of you are still shopping for my Christmas present, please get me one that is finished. I've decided that my favourite word in the English language is 'pre-assembled'.

Erma Bombeck

The three great holiday gift lies are: 'Easy to assemble', 'Unbreakable', and 'One size fits all'.

Pat Williams

I was the worst gift buyer as a child. When I was 13 my sister gave me an LP and a birdhouse, and in return I gave her one of those big-value, one-litre bottles of shampoo. I think it was 20p.

Ricky Gervais

We gave our presents on Christmas morning between opening our stockings and church. Nancy once despised my present so much that she threw it straight on the fire. Strangely enough I did not mind a bit; I knew it was a hopeless present and admired her courage in demonstrating her displeasure.

Diana Mitford

I bought my brother some gift-wrap for Christmas. I took it to the Gift Wrap department and told them to wrap it, but in a different print so he knows when to stop unwrapping.

Steven Wright

A couple of years ago I'd left my gift buying to the last minute, so I bought my relatives and their kids ten quids' worth of scratch cards. One of them won 17 quid, but some of the younger children didn't win anything. So that was a valuable life lesson: 'Some people are winners, some are losers.'

Ricky Gervais

Things I Hate About Christmas: Presents. If I like people enough, I will give them gifts when I want to. The annual manic marathon around department stores is not my idea of heaven on earth. And in exchange for all this effort, gallons of after-shave and miles of nylon socks that take an entire year to burn, bury or otherwise divest.

Iain Grant

My son has a big Christmas problem – what do you buy for a father who has everything and you're using it?

Milton Berle

My True Love Gave to Me

The race to get a Christmas present for Father usually ends in a tie.

Gene Shalit

There ought to be technical education classes on the science of present giving. No one seems to have the faintest notion of what anyone else wants, and the prevalent ideas on the subject are not creditable to a civilized community. There is, for instance, the female relative in the country who 'knows a tie is always useful', and sends you some spotted horror that you could only wear in secret or in Tottenham Court Road. It might have been useful had she kept it to tie up currant bushes with, when it would have served the double purpose of supporting the branches and frightening away the birds – for it is an admitted fact that the ordinary tomtit of commerce has a sounder aesthetic taste than the average female relative in the country.

Saki, Reginald on Christmas Presents

Over Christmas lunch I gave Daddy a huge present which I'd wrapped up at the flat. He opened it with glee. In it were six bottles of champagne that Leslie Grade had given me. I'd seen nothing wrong in rewrapping them for Daddy. I'd put a card inside. 'Thank you, Pussycat …' He bent forward to butt me with his forehead when his hand touched something else. He pulled out another card and read, 'To dearest Sarah. Happy Christmas! Love, Leslie Grade.' Father never let that one go.

Sarah Miles

Presents were varied. Dad [Roald Dahl] would wrap mine in a bit of newspaper and 'chuck' it at me. As he didn't use Sellotape, by the time it landed it didn't need unwrapping. For as many years as I care to admit I never managed to steel myself for his lack of enthusiasm as he unwrapped my

present to him. Thank God my mother's throaty, delighted
joy counteracted his gruff loathing of all emotion which
came gift-wrapped.

Tessa Dahl

– What Christmas gift did you get your girlfriend?
– I gave her the best gift on earth: I let her date me.
Priceless.
– Well, I guess, if you like used gifts …

Jay Leno and Simon Cowell

Then there are aunts. They are always a difficult class to deal
with in the matter of presents. The trouble is that one never
catches them really young enough. By the time one has
educated them to an appreciation of the fact that one does
not wear red woollen mittens in the West End, they die, or
quarrel with the family, or do something equally
inconsiderate. That is why the supply of trained aunts is
always so precarious.

Saki, Reginald on Christmas Presents

Then there's the points-for-trouble-taken system used by
wives on your present to them, whereby a diamond
necklace scores zero if ordered by telephone and paid for
through the post, with something like a maximum score for
a Cannibal Island nose-ring obtained on the spot in person,
though in practice they'll usually settle for quite a humble
object provided you get it after a couple of days' trudging
around town.

Kingsley Amis

Christmas itself was quite good. Got Jane a gold bar in her
stocking.

Alan Clark, MP

My True Love Gave to Me

One should never give a woman anything she can't wear in the evening.

Oscar Wilde

Christmas is the time of year when we all become really good at lying ... Last year my mother should have at least received a Best Actress nomination for her performance after receiving the shoe-tree my aunt gave her.

Ellen DeGeneres

Emerald says she is bored with Christianity, and all its festivals, Christmas especially, which she says is 'only for servants'. But she graciously accepts a green Sèvres vase cup – circa 1775 – which we bought her.

Sir Henry 'Chips' Channon

Personally, I can't see where the difficulty in choosing suitable presents lies. No boy who had brought himself up properly could fail to appreciate one of those decorative bottles of liqueurs ... And then, of course, there are liqueur glasses, and crystallized fruits, and tapestry curtains and heaps of other necessaries of life that make really sensible presents – not to speak of luxuries, such as having one's bills paid, or getting something quite sweet in the way of jewellery. Unlike the alleged Good Woman of the Bible, I'm not above rubies.

Saki, Reginald on Christmas Presents

More diamonds are bought at Christmas (31 per cent) than for any other event of the year.

Keith Waterhouse

It's widely known that one of the reasons I gave up drinking was to avoid having to go to the pub on Christmas Day. The sight of 25 men creating a sea of static electricity with their just-unwrapped, absurdly patterned sweaters is not consistent with good cheer.

A. A. Gill

Some friends of mine got me a sweater. I'd have preferred a moaner or a screamer, but the sweater was OK.

Steven Wright

A woman in a Christmas sweater has something to tell us about herself, something not so different from the man who shows up on casual Fridays wearing a Hawaiian shirt, and what they're both telling us is this: Watch out, I feel festive … She has transported herself to another dimension, a place of the pleasantly snowy, post-Victorian, sentimentally charged, in fact non-existent kountry kristmas, for which she has been readying herself all year. For ever, really.

Hank Stuever

The wife of a man who never learnt the difference between a brassière and a brazier was granted a divorce today on two counts. First because when she wanted underwear for Christmas he gave her two big rusty tins with holes in and second because of the way he kept trying to roast his chestnuts.

Ronnie Barker

My girlfriend seems to forget the money I spent on her. Christmas, for example, I bought her six pairs of stockings. And later, for her birthday, I had all the stockings darned.

Groucho Marx

The best stocking-filler is a shapely leg.

Anon

My True Love Gave to Me

You know you're getting old when everything you want for Christmas can be purchased at a drugstore.

Pat Williams

Unreturnable, unusable, unsightly and unfun. These are just some of the words you can use to describe home-made gifts. Even grandmas secretly hate them, but they have to pretend they love multicoloured, glitter-covered macaroni sculptures. They just want a DVD player like everyone else.

Ellen DeGeneres

Christmas Craft Fair: Buying someone a dressed wooden spoon, because you feel you ought to be doing something for the post-industrial society.

Malcolm Burgess

[*In school pottery class*] With their thick clumsy bases, my mugs weighed in at close to five pounds each. I gave my mother a matching set for Christmas, and she accepted them as graciously as possible, announcing that they would make perfect pet bowls. The mugs were set on the kitchen floor and remained there until the cat chipped a tooth and went on hunger-strike.

David Sedaris, Me Talk Pretty Some Day

I remember the year I received my first 'crumb scraper'. It was fashioned from half a paper plate and a lace doily. I have never seen such shining pride from my little four-year-old girl who asked, 'You don't have one already, do you?' ... I still receive gifts at Christmas. They are thoughtful. They are wrapped with care. They are what I need. But oh, how I wish I could bend low and receive a gift of cardboard and paste so that I could hear the chimes ring at Christmas just once more.

Erma Bombeck

— Oh, Homey, look at that watch. I've always wanted a watch like that.

— Well, maybe someone will give you one for Christmas. [*Thinking*] Now she'll *really* be surprised when she opens that ironing board cover.

Marge and Homer Simpson, The Simpsons

Life is like hoping for a racing bike for Christmas, and getting a Spirograph.

Lynne Truss

The most splendid Christmas gift, the most marvelled and magic, is the gift that has not yet been opened.

Gregg Easterbrook

According to Bill Bryson, Christmas in America is a dull affair that ends at midday, when people start returning unwanted presents to the stores. Being behind America in these matters, we have to wait until Boxing Day.

Anthony Sattin

You can tell if someone doesn't like the gift you have given them if they say, 'I love it.' If they say they love it you can be sure they hate it. Loving a towel rack makes no sense, so clearly they're overcompensating for the feelings of guilt and shame, for the deeper feelings of anger and resentment they have about being given a towel rack for Christmas.

Ellen DeGeneres

The first thing my family says when they open gifts is, 'Have you got the receipt?'

Jenny Eclair

Christmas Parties

The best Christmas gift of all is the presence of a happy
family all wrapped up with one another.

E. C. McKenzie

My rule of thumb for Christmas-like occasions is to try to
acknowledge my own ambivalent feelings, and to develop
low expectations … One family I heard of had an even
better suggestion. Each member was to have their own little
foil-wrapped gift on the Christmas tree. In it lay a bottle of
Valium.

Ann Karpf

The only gift is a portion of thyself.

Ralph Waldo Emerson

There are all kinds of presents one can get for Christmas.
The best is love.

Helen Hayes

Christmas Parties

One quick drink, that's all they're getting. Then it's happy
Christmas and out they bloody well go.

Geoffrey, Absurd Person Singular

Can I refill your eggnog for you? Get you something to
eat? Drive you out to the middle of nowhere and leave you
for dead?

Clark Griswold, Christmas Vacation

Family parties? Friends' ones? Just the same, i.e. just the
same as last Yule's, give or take the odd divorce or
headstone, what's your son doing, mine's doing this, how

was Tuscany, Provence was great, did you change cars, nor
did I, is your hernia still playing up, I must sort out this
bloody cartilage, what about the Budget, then, what about
QPR?

Alan Coren

I have only been to one. It was four years ago, where I had
to dress up as a man because Mary was there.

*Sally Farmiloe, former mistress of Jeffrey Archer,
on his famous Christmas parties*

Supped at the Club D'Elysée with Marlene Dietrich and
Ginette, and it was gay and sweet and terribly exciting, and
we were joined by Burt Bacharach and got into a discussion
about crabs. Marlene sorrowfully announced that she had
once had them for Christmas.

Noël Coward

Christmas in Britain these days is almost completely ruined
by the office party. The streets become full of ordinary
people who have suddenly lost the ability to walk in a
straight line. And the atmosphere in every restaurant is
firebombed by the table of 60 who order food not for its
taste but its aerodynamic efficiency.

Jeremy Clarkson

[Christmas] is about breaking the mini-sausage roll of peace
with your boss at the office party, drinking vast quantities of
Piat d'Or from white plastic cups, then a couple of hours
later pushing people out of the way in your haste to
photocopy your bottom.

Marian Keyes

For a fortnight before the big day life becomes unbearable,
as traffic gets worse, shops get more crowded, and habitually
abstemious office girls unwisely accept a glass or six of

Christmas Parties

Bailey's at the Christmas party and are later discovered in a
Y-shape underneath the under-manager in the stationery
cupboard, anything but stationary.

Victor Lewis-Smith

On no account should you wear a red velvet smoking
jacket. People will laugh at you.

Dylan Jones

The Treasury Christmas lunch was a fairly hard slog. The
Financial Secretary entertained his staff at Joe Allen's, which
was an ideal venue because the din and clatter were so great
no one could hear anybody and the fact that nobody
seemed to have much to say to anybody consequently
didn't matter. Stephen [Dorrell] is delightful ... but
slumming it with the troops, small talk with the secretaries,
seasonal banter with the lower ranks – these are not his
forte.

Gyles Brandreth, Breaking the Code

Christmas is already causing considerable anxiety. I often
think of running away to a country hotel for a few days in
the hope that it might be vaguely Dickensian but the reality
would be rooms full of yuppies wearing silly paper hats.

Jeffrey Bernard

When past a certain age, a man wearing a paper hat in a
public restaurant looks absurd, and that age is earlier than
most men seem to think.

Lord Deedes

Best Excuse for Not Coming to a Mirror *Lunch.* Michael
Green, the TV mogul: 'Dear Piers, it is with huge regret I
have decided to miss your Christmas lunch and instead fly
to the Maldives, first class, with people I love, and not have a

care in the world. If my mobile works, I promise to send pictures.'

Piers Morgan

The worst job I ever had was working the photocopier at the bus station. I was the only one at the Christmas party.

Steven Wright

A survey this week revealed that 45 per cent of people have had it away at the works Christmas do. Why? You sit opposite the plump girl for 48 weeks and it never once occurs to you that she is interesting. So how come, after one warm wine, she only needs to put on a paper hat to become Jordan?

Jeremy Clarkson

Some people get terribly po-faced when talking about couples who disappear into the office filing cabinet together. But speaking as someone who has seen more than a couple of pencil sharpeners under cover of darkness, I can testify that it's fun – provided you preserve some modicum of discretion. Those amateurs who ignore this caveat are often left with faces redder than Rudolph's nose. How about the couple I heard of who retired to a City boardroom for a festive fumble, but forgot that the security cameras were keeping watch?

Virginia Blackburn

The most intelligent garment for a girl to wear to an office party is a wet suit.

Jilly Cooper

At the Christmas office party, you're supposed to sit naked on the photocopy machine, not the shredder.

David Letterman

Christmas Parties

Do not be tempted to do it on the photocopier. Not even in an ironic way. The manufacturer Canon last year confirmed that it has had to increase the thickness of its glass to cope with an alarming number of bottom-related breakages. A third of Canon technicians say that they have had to mend machines that have been sat on.

Julie Fisher

Another awful thing about these Christmas parties can be coming face to face with a hackette or secretary that you featured with 20 years ago. Embarrassing for both parties but less so for the one with the worse memory. There are women who have etched in their eyes the unspoken question, 'Why didn't you telephone?'

Jeffrey Bernard

Christmas is a time when everybody wants his past forgotten and his present remembered. What I don't like about office Christmas parties is looking for a job the next day.

Phyllis Diller

Please welcome the late arrivals at the Christmas ball: Mr and Mrs Amanger, and their son, Wayne; Mr and Mrs Donionstuffing, and their very wise daughter, 'Sage' Ann; Mr and Mrs Eltoe, and their daughter, Miss Eltoe – Oh, there's someone under her! Mr and Mrs Even, and their pizza-making son, Deep-pan Crispian; from Mexico, Mr and Mrs Horse-Opensleigh, and their son, Juan.

I'm Sorry I Haven't a Clue radio show

Believe it or not, our Christmas menu is now available and we are taking bookings. Sorry!

Sign in an East Sussex pub, July 2005

Love Came Down at Christmas

Blessed is the season which engages the whole world in a conspiracy of love.

Hamilton Wright Mabie

Nothing during the year is so impressively convincing as the vision Christmas brings of what this world would be if love became the daily practice of human beings.

Norman Vincent Peale

Probably the reason we all go so haywire at Christmas time with the endless unrestrained and often silly buying of gifts is that we don't quite know how to put our love into words.

Harlan Miller

> The Summer hath his joyes,
> And Winter his delights;
> Though Love and all his pleasures are but toyes,
> They shorten tedious nights.

Thomas Campion

Rose late – dull and drooping – the weather dripping and dense. Snow on the ground, and sirocco above in the sky, like yesterday. Roads up to the horse's belly, so that riding (at least for pleasure) is not very feasible. Read the conclusion for the fiftieth time (I have read all W. Scott's novels at least fifty times), of the third series of *Tales of My Landlord* – grand work – Scotch.

Clock strikes – going out to make love. Somewhat perilous, but not disagreeable …

Lord Byron

Love Came Down at Christmas

Ill–conceived love is like a Christmas cracker – one massively disappointing bang, and the novelty soon wears off.

Ebenezer Blackadder, Blackadder's Christmas Carol

I'm going to attach a pine cone to my vibrator and have a really merry Christmas!

Bobbi Markowitz, The Stepford Wives

When I was a child in Cork, we didn't have a lot of money. There was no Christmas tree, no decorations, no turkey, no mince pies, no crackers – yet my parents had astonishing generosity. I remember the presents at the end of the bed, the highlight always being the Christmas annual. The first I can remember was Rupert the Bear. I did not feel deprived as a child because we were living in love. I still believe in the midst of all this plenty that what is most important is that we have succeeded in giving our children love in the family.

George Hook

My idea of Christmas, whether old–fashioned or modern, is very simple: loving others. Come to think of it, why do we have to wait for Christmas to do that?

Bob Hope

Christmas is most truly Christmas when we celebrate it by giving the light of love to those who need it most.

Ruth Carter Stapleton

Christmas is about a love that will not let us down and will not let us go, but which can never be bought.

Reverend John Wynburne

It is Christmas every time you let God love others through you … yes, it is Christmas every time you smile at your brother and offer him your hand.

Mother Teresa

I Saw Mommy Kissing Santa Claus: Mistletoe Etiquette

– Are you going to kiss me under this mistletoe?
– I wouldn't kiss you under an anaesthetic.

Maud Grimes and Percy Sugden, Coronation Street

If you are ever in doubt as to whether or not you should kiss a pretty girl, always give her the benefit of the doubt.

Thomas Carlyle

I'm not saying the wife's mother is ugly, but last Christmas she stood under the mistletoe waiting for someone to kiss her and she was still stood there at Lent.

Les Dawson

Always be prepared for a mistletoe ambush. Carry a can of mace spray.

Christopher Douglas and Mick Newman,
Mastering the Universe radio show

At a family Christmas gathering … the kissing … was liberal and included eight under-fives who didn't want to be kissed and whom I didn't want to touch with a bargepole, let alone my mouth (all that dried-on snot and chocolate biscuit debris). But to have refused would be to have branded myself a stony-hearted child-hater. So I took a deep breath and got stuck in.

Judy Rumbold

Few men know how to kiss well; fortunately, I've always had time to teach them.

Mae West

Christmas Wisecracks

You have to kiss an awful lot of frogs before you find a prince.

Anon

Kissing don't last; cookery do!

George Meredith

Christmas Wisecracks

Everybody's got the Christmas spirit here in New York. The pickpockets won't take your watch unless it's gift-wrapped.

Bob Hope

—Why is Christmas just like a day at the office?
—You do all the work and the fat guy in the suit gets all the credit.

Anon

Sex is like snow. You never know how many inches you're going to get or how long it will last.

Anon

I used to be Snow White, but I drifted.

Mae West

I'm as pure as the driven slush.

Tallulah Bankhead

Family Christmas

I think the real miracle of Christmas is how I get through it each year without killing my relatives.

Reno Goodale

The older I get the more I loathe Christmas, because now I have a horrible family of my own to add to the one who previously scarred me for life.

Jenny Eclair

— But, Dad, why can't I go skiing with my friends? A lot of people I like are going to be there.
— Christmas is not about being with people you like. It's about being with your family.

Brad and Tim Taylor, Home Improvement

If God had meant Christmas to be a family occasion, he wouldn't have invented television, would he?

Rory McGrath

Thirteen Irritating Things People Do at Christmas. 1) Tell you you can always take it back and change it if you don't like it. 2) Bustle around asking where the forks go. 3) Make a show of singing louder on the third 'O come let us adore him'. 4) Mingle. 5) Insist on trying to revive the art of conversation. 6) Say 'Bah, humbug' in a jocular voice. 7) Say 'Oh, but you shouldn't have'. 8) Forget the bread sauce. 9) Keep reminding everyone that Christmas is for the kids. 10) Tidy away the wrapping paper the second it comes off each present. 11) Encourage you to join in a sing-song. 12) Invite you round to meet the new people who have just moved in at number 15. 13) Repeat cracker jokes.

Craig Brown

The worst part of Christmas is dinner with the family, when you realize how truly mutated and crippled is the gene stock from which you sprang.

P.J. O'Rourke

Christmas, that time of year when people descend into the bunker of the family.

Byron Rogers

Family Christmas

What I like is the way that extended family Christmases take on all the traditions brought by each separate family and add them to the rest. So my wife's family like a nice cold glass of Bailey's while opening presents, while others we'll be with tomorrow will have their eye on something sparkling. Then there will be mince pies, a couple of those mini–Toblerone things, like chocolate shrapnel, and before lunch no doubt a spot of smoked salmon.

Simon Hoggart

A Family Christmas: Also known as Ayckbournesque.

Malcolm Burgess

Season's Greetings is a play about love and about ... how unfair it all is. And success and failure. And jealousy and self-deception. And greed and envy and lust and gluttony. Just an average family Christmas.

Alan Ayckbourn

Christmases in my house were like a Hammer horror version of *Big Brother*. Four mismatched individuals, with nothing more in common than a few strands of DNA, trapped under the same roof, the action fuelled by drink, paranoia and dyspepsia.

Sarah Vine

A traditional Christmas with all the trimmings: sulking, moping, hurt feelings with perhaps the odd migraine, nosebleed and suppurating gravy-pan burn thrown into the festive pot.

Christopher Douglas and Mick Newman,
Mastering the Universe radio show

Everyone's gonna fight, call each other bastards, and go to bed early.

Sharon Osbourne

... above all, Christmas is about rows. Terrible rows. Shocking, unexpected rows. Caused partly by the huge expectations of Christmas and what it actually delivers. And partly by there being too many self-governing autonomous adults crammed into one house, having to obey someone else's rules and follow someone else's routine. (I also blame the central heating being up too high.)

Marian Keyes

Most common causes of Christmas Day rows

- When to open the presents.
- When to have lunch.
- When the kids can leave the table to go back to the television.
- Kids eating an entire selection box by 9 a.m.
- Someone using all the tonic water as a soft drink.
- Children trying to play with each other's toys.
- Dad being too busy to assemble a complicated toy.
- Dad interfering in the assembly of a complicated toy.
- Kisses under the mistletoe which are too passionate.

You Magazine

One of the biggest rows I ever had began and ended soon after one Christmas Day morning with my mother-in-law triumphantly sweeping out of my house and victoriously declaring, as though it was a bullet through my heart, 'You must be a very unhappy man.' Not to see the end of her, I wasn't, but I did cry later on that very cold day when I saw that not only had I run out of wives but logs too.

Jeffrey Bernard

We are having the same old thing for Christmas dinner this year ... relatives.

Mark Twain

Family Christmas

We're always together at Christmas, even that year your father fell down the chimney. We were in the emergency room, but we were together.

Jill Taylor, Home Improvement

The great thing about having kids on Christmas Day is that you get up, open their stockings, go downstairs, open their presents, have a leisurely breakfast, have a shower, get dressed and it's still only a quarter past six.

Fred Macaulay

The gifts aren't the important thing about Christmas. The important thing is having your family around resenting you.

Reno Goodale

My family, when I was a child, specialized in unhappy Christmases. By the time I was 19 I had seen Christmases disrupted by violence, acrimony, infidelity and mean-spiritedness – often all at the same time. Christmas dinners were frigid affairs where everyone spent minutes examining the tines of their forks, just in case another family member made a lunge.

Will Self

I don't really enjoy Christmas very much and I often feel a sense of relief when its all over. This goes back to my childhood when several turned out to be pretty disappointing. Our family was very small and Christmas Day could be rather tense and unpleasant. I often chose to go out bird-watching instead and still have notebooks written when I was an early teenager, which say things like: 'Went out bird-watching on Christmas Day. Left them arguing about who was going to burn the sprouts.'

Bill Oddie

Family Christmas

Happy Christmases are all alike; every unhappy Christmas is unhappy in its own way.

Ann Patchett

I hate a family gathering at Christmas. What does it mean? Why, someone says: 'Ah! we miss poor Uncle James who was here last year,' and we all begin to snivel. Someone else says: 'It's two years since poor Aunt Liz used to sit in that corner.' Then we all begin to snivel again. Then another gloomy relation says: 'Ah! I wonder whose turn it will be next?' Then we all snivel again, and proceed to eat and drink too much; and they don't discover until *I* get up that we have been seated thirteen at dinner.

George Grossmith, The Diary of a Nobody

I've had so many wives and so many children I don't know which house to go to first on Christmas.

Mickey Rooney, eight times married

I'll be doling out turkey and vegetarian alternatives to my children, their father, my boyfriend, my mother, my sisters, one sister's ex-boyfriend, my ex-sister-in-law, her former partner, my ex-husband's stepmother and his half-sister (I hate the word half-sister – you're either someone's sister or you aren't), plus assorted old friends, new ones and the odd lame duck.

India Knight

I'm so bad at relationships. I haven't made a holiday twice with the same person. I have a box full of pictures of *Our First Christmas Together*.

Michele Balan

Family Christmas

It's one of the things about being an adulteress all my life.
Christmas is one time of the year when I'm left strictly
alone – because he'd be elsewhere attending to his family.

Germaine Greer

You know you're in California when you invite your
analyst to Christmas lunch.

Anon

[Christmas at Sandringham] was fairly fraught. Isn't that
awful? I can't remember what people bought me. I do all
the presents and Prince Charles signs the cards. [It was]
terrifying and so disappointing. No boisterous behaviour,
lots of tension, silly behaviour, silly jokes that outsiders
would find odd but insiders understood.

Diana, Princess of Wales

Q: As usual, Emma is dreading spending Christmas with her
parents, just as much as she dreads it when she spends it
with her in-laws. How can she make Christmas better?
A: Have you ever wondered whether your parents and in-
laws dread *you* coming to stay for Christmas?

The Independent

Christmas is a time when you get homesick – even when
you're home.

Carol Nelson

Sophie [my daughter] and her boyfriend invited me to stay
in his lovely, warm, calm, un-neurotic house. It was a time
of real joy, enhanced by the baggy pyjamas we were all
given on Christmas Eve with instructions that we had to
follow his Christmas tradition of wearing pj's all day. I plan
to implement this custom myself now, and highly
recommend you do, too.

Tessa Dahl

Every year on Christmas Day I like to tell my mother that I'm a lesbian, even though I'm not. It just gets everything going.

Jenny Eclair

A great psychiatric paper could be written on parental remarks at the Christmas lunch table that drive their children to the edge of the abyss, unnoticed by anyone else present.

Philip Norman

Every aunt, if fed enough liquor, becomes amusing. If not, pour yourself more liquor.

Grace Bradberry

We're fast approaching that special moment at Christmas when Granddad's had too much to drink. We don't call him Granddad, we just call him Alcopops.

Jimmy Carr

Christmas is being together – gathering together. It is the time of the heart's inventory. It is the time of going home in many ways.

William Saroyan

How to survive Christmas: Tell the in-laws you're spending Christmas Day with your parents. Tell your parents you're spending Christmas Day with the in-laws. Tell everyone else you're going away.

You Magazine

Christmas Eve

Oh, joy, Christmas Eve! By this time tomorrow, millions of
people, knee-deep in tinsel and wrapping paper, will utter
those heartfelt words, 'Is this all I got?'

Frasier Crane, Cheers

William is now sitting by me, at half past 10 o'clock. I have
been beside him ever since tea running the heel of a stocking,
repeating some of his sonnets to him, reading some of
Milton's and the *Allegro* and *Penseroso*. It is quite keen frost.
   Mary is in the parlour below attending to the baking of
cakes and Jenny Fletcher's pies. Sara is in bed with the
tooth-ache …

Dorothy Wordsworth

Christmas Eve dinner for George Weidenfeld, Min Hogg,
John and Miriam Gross … The Grosses were later found on
our bed, an exceptionally anti-social thing for a husband
and wife to do. There was later a quiz of my composition
(identifying famous tits and bottoms, privately recorded
voices of the famous and less famous revolutionary
quotations) with champagne prizes. A memorable evening.

Kenneth Tynan, Diaries

Buy a pair of red flannel pyjamas that you wear only on
Christmas Eve.

H. Jackson Brown, Jr

'On Christmas Eve,' I thought, as a child, 'even the furniture
looks different!' The chests and cupboards, tables and chairs
of my nursery shed on me, possibly, no more than the good
nature which was in them always: I simply was more open
to it that night.

Elizabeth Bowen

Christmas Eve

Everything was fine, in the way that it is on Christmas Eve when you're a kid and the shapes of the packages under the tree are just right and you only have to wait till morning to open them.

Elizabeth Hartley Winthrop

'Twas the night before Christmas,
when all through the house
Not a creature was stirring,
not even a mouse;
the stockings were hung
by the chimney with care,
In hopes that St Nicholas
soon would be there.

Clement C. Moore

This is the hour, unique in the whole year, of Christmas Eve. It is always the same and always different.

Pearl S. Buck

On Christmas Eve, the whole house used to tingle with suppressed excitement.

Bing Crosby

In some parts of England bees are popularly said to express the veneration of the Nativity by singing, as it is called, in their hives at midnight on Christmas Eve.

John N. Then

Never work for a liberal employer. They'll sack you on Christmas Eve.

Philip Hope-Wallace

Peace on earth and mercy mild are still possible. On Christmas Eve, all things are possible.

Gregg Easterbrook

Christmas Day

Christmas! The very word brings joy to our hearts. No matter how we may dread the rush, the long Christmas lists for gifts and cards to be bought and given – when Christmas Day comes there is still the same warm feeling we had as children, the same warmth that enfolds our hearts and our homes.

Joan Winmill Brown

No fog, no mist; clear, bright, jovial, stirring, cold; cold, piping for the blood to dance to; Golden sunlight; Heavenly sky; sweet fresh air; merry bells. Oh, glorious. Glorious!

Charles Dickens, A Christmas Carol

Christmas Day itself was organized by Lady Bobbin with the thoroughness and attention to detail of a general leading his army into battle.

Nancy Mitford

As I lay praying in the early morning I thought I heard a sound of distant bells. It was an intense frost. I sat down in my bath upon a sheet of thick ice which broke in the middle into large pieces whilst the sharp points and jagged edges stuck all round the side of the tub like chevaux de frise, not particularly comfortable to the naked thighs and loins, because the keen ice cut like broken glass. The ice water stung and scorched like fire. I had to collect the floating pieces of ice and pile them on a chair before I could use the sponge and then I had to thaw the sponge in my hands for it was a mass of ice. The morning was most brilliant. Walked to the Sunday School with Gibbons and the road sparkled with millions of rainbows, the seven colours gleaming in every glittering point of hoar-frost. The Church was very cold in spite of two roaring fires.

Reverend Francis Kilvert

... a few home truths about Christmas in the countryside: Contrary to Christmas card lore, it doesn't always snow on Christmas Day. Nor does a coach and horses stop outside the local pub; the large brown quadrupeds with horns are roe deer, not reindeer; a Christmas Day walk is compulsory unless it clashes with the Queen's Speech or the James Bond film; do not drink from bottles with the hand-written label 'Home Farm Sloe Gin' or similar.

Adam Edwards

A peaceful Christmas Day spent in bed talking to people on the telephone. Sybil, Graham, Gladys and I had dinner. Delicious food, including caviar. Later, a party at Binkie's. Very enjoyable.

Noël Coward

Got up and it was Sunday. Tried to dye my eyebrows and my hair. I wasn't in the mood. Got not too many phone calls. Actually none, I guess ... Tried to wrap presents ... Watched a lot of terrible TV.

Andy Warhol

A Christmas Day, to be perfect, should be clear and cold, with holly branches in berry, a blazing fire, a dinner with mince pies, and games and forfeits in the evening. You cannot have it in perfection if you are very fine and fashionable.

Leigh Hunt

One doesn't forget the rounded wonder in the eyes of a boy as he comes bursting upstairs on Christmas morning and finds the two-wheeler or the fire truck of which for weeks he scarcely dared dream.

Max Lerner

Christmas Day

Isn't Christmas Day a long day? ... I know it's the same as any other day – but oh, it does seem like a long day.

Barbara Royle, The Royle Family

In the afternoon, do you go for a walk, stuffed and bundled-up, staring dully at the children with new skateboards and the unaccountably happy dogs? Do you watch the Queen's broadcast, wondering if anyone gave her a balsawood pestle and mortar? Do you play games of Trivial Pursuit and Give Us a Clue? Do you remember Raymond Chandler's line about time passing 'at the speed of a sick cockroach'?

Philip Norman

At about 4 p.m. on Christmas Day I always wish I was somewhere else. The combination of dry sherry, dryer turkey and the sight of David Jason churning out another eight-hour *Only Fools and Horses* special turns any goodwill I started the day with into bitterness – and don't get me started on the in-laws. By 6 p.m. I'm usually hiding out in my shed, drunk on self-pity.

Christian O'Connell

Christmas Day nightmares

- Cooking sherry before lunch.
- Being sent out to find a shop which is open and sells batteries.
- Someone buying the kids a Little Drummer kit.
- Still waiting for the turkey to defrost at 5 p.m.
- 'Fun' underwear.
- Getting stuck with the dark meat.
- Being forced to wear the hat out of your cracker.
- Someone counting the 'units' of alcohol you've had.

You Magazine

By keeping the children in bed for long periods we managed to have a tolerable Christmas Day. My only present, a very welcome one, a box of cigars from Auberon. I have seats for both Bath and Bristol pantomimes. The children leave on the 10th. Meanwhile I have my meals in the library.

Evelyn Waugh

I always make a point of a long London walk on Christmas Day, savouring the stilled city, free for once of its traffic and commerce. This in itself is enough of a present for me – all the rest is gravy.

Will Self

A Christmas evening should, if possible, finish with music. It carries off the excitement without abruptness, and sheds a repose over the conclusion of the enjoyment.

Leigh Hunt

Talking Turkey: Christmas Fare

Only 89 days left until Christmas, so it's now time to put your Brussels sprouts on the hob to boil, and make the Christmas pudding, with coins secreted in the mixture.

Victor Lewis-Smith

This year I have two friends coming for lunch and this time I shall take it easy in the morning and try to remember to put some water in the saucepan of sprouts. Last year they were brown and hard and looked like roast chestnuts.

Jeffrey Bernard

Talking Turkey

We've got our Christmas dinner already cooking. Spent two hours trussing up that lump of corned beef.

Tony Hancock, Hancock's Half Hour

I trust Christmas brings to you its traditional mix of good food and violent stomach cramp.

Ebenezer Blackadder, Blackadder's Christmas Carol

... Christmas dinner – the single most disgusting meal ever invented, with the exception of American Thanksgiving ... Nobody sane or loving could invent Christmas food from scratch.

A. A. Gill

The basic Christmas spread is the dullest meal of the year to a generation who've eaten Thai green curries in provincial pubs by the age of nine.

Peter York

Hugh Fearnley-Whittingstall's *A River Cottage Christmas Feast* involves a woodcock cooked inside a pigeon, inside a pheasant, inside a duck, inside a goose, inside a turkey. This was first shown last year, so it will be a repeat, and in more senses than one for anyone reckless enough to eat this motorway pile-up of poultry.

Paul Hoggart

Put a pigeon in a partridge in a wild duck in a pheasant in a capon in a goose in a turkey – and that'll feed 50.

Clarissa Dickson Wright

Christmas? Christmas means dinner, dinner means death! Death means carnage; Christmas means carnage!

Ferdinand the Duck, Babe

Talking Turkey

One turkey will enjoy Christmas dinner this year after being saved from the chop by a duchess. The turkey, named Ankara, fell off a lorry heading for a slaughterhouse in Fife and has now been adopted as a pet by the Duchess of Hamilton, a well-known animal lover. The duchess is not a meat eater and said yesterday that, in any event, good manners dictated that she could 'never eat anything I had been introduced to'.

Shirley English

Christmas is the one time of year when gluttony is a sin everyone is guilty of. Excess is the order of the day – and I love it. When I was a child, for Christmas dinner we always had smoked salmon, a turkey raised on corn and milk, and 14 pounds of fine York ham. My brother and I were delegated to prepare the brandy butter. It was a matter of pride to see if we could blend a whole bottle of brandy into a pound of butter. As there were usually only eight of us for the meal, there was plenty to go round.

Clarissa Dickson Wright

What with Christmas just around the corner and the nights drawing in, I wondered if you'd considered the benefits of saving for a Yuletide hamper? Consolidate all your festive shopping into one manageable chunk and banish those trips to the supermarket. Never mind about normal food. We've packed our hamper full of food you'll never normally dream of buying in a million years. Tins of ham and strange relishes are just the starting point, as you discover the joys of non-mainstream foodstuffs, and sample things you thought were no longer made. Mrs Bloggins of Luton had this to say: 'My hamper was a lifesaver. Without it, my Christmas wouldn't have been worth celebrating.' So, buy now on a no win, no fee basis. Even the dog can do it. No salesman will call. And when you order, we'll give you a free gift to welcome you.

Sandy Claus, 'Hampers R Us'

Talking Turkey

*Ten Unpleasant Surprises to be Found in Luxury
Christmas Hampers*

1) Glace Cherries in Chocolate. 2) Organic Aubergine and
Gherkin Luxury Spread. 3) Sun-Dried Tomatoes in an
Artichoke Marinade. 4) Caramelized Yoghurt-Coated
Macadamia Nuts Dipped in Luxury Belgian Chocolate.
5) Port and Stilton Chutney. 6) Smoked Salmon in Madeira.
7) Old-Fashioned Rhubarb and Liquorice Boiled Sweets.
8) Luxury Organic Boiled Egg Ice-Cream. 9) Turkish
Delight. 10) Ginger, Mango, Partridge and Gorgonzola Pâté.

Craig Brown

At Ambergate my sister had sent a motor car for us – so we
were at Ripley in time for turkey and Christmas pudding.
My God, what masses of food here, turkey, large tongues,
long wall of roast loin of pork, pork pies, sausages, mince
pies, dark cakes covered with almonds, cheesecakes, lemon
tarts, jellies, endless masses of food, with whisky, gin, port
wine, burgundy, muscatel. It seems incredible.

D. H. Lawrence

The most indulgent Christmas spread ever was one that my
fellow 'Fat Lady', Jennifer Paterson, and I prepared for the
'cost-cutting' former head of the BBC, John Birt, as he
entertained the board of governors. We watched them
indulge in goose stuffed with foie gras and a Christmas
pudding bombe made with vintage brandy butter.

Clarissa Dickson Wright

[My ultimate food moment] was Christmas lunch in South
Africa in the late 1960s, the last one I would spend with my
parents. We dangled our feet in the Palmiet River and ate
cold turkey salad and Christmas pudding fried in butter. It
was absolutely the best Christmas meal.

Sue MacGregor

Don't count calories from December 17th to January 2nd.

H. Jackson Brown, Jr

Several years ago we found ourselves dealing with a
Christmas lunch for 22. Carrying a trestle table a mile from
the village hall was nothing compared with the ingenuity
required in the culinary department. The large turkey
occupied all the available oven space, the hobs were
required for vegetables, but what about the ham? Answer –
the Hotpoint twin tub, set to boil. No one was any the
wiser; it carved well and tasted superb.

Nick Reid

At last the dishes were set on, and grace was said. It was
succeeded by a breathless pause, as Mrs Cratchit, looking
slowly all along the carving-knife, prepared to plunge it in
the breast; but when she did, and when the long expected
gush of stuffing issued forth, one murmur of delight arose
all round the board, and even Tiny Tim, excited by the two
young Cratchits, beat on the table with the handle of his
knife, and feebly cried 'Hurrah!'

Charles Dickens, A Christmas Carol

A Christmas dinner, with the middle classes of this empire,
would scarcely be a Christmas dinner without its turkey;
and we can hardly imagine an object of greater envy than is
presented by a respected, portly paterfamilias carving, at the
season devoted to good cheer and genial charity, his own fat
turkey, and carving it well.

Mrs Isabella Beeton

Each year, newspapers print instructions on how to cook a
turkey, as if they were telling you how to personally install
central heating in your home over the two-day holiday.

Joe Joseph

Talking Turkey

How to thaw a frozen turkey: blow in its ear.

Johnny Carson

The turkey should be cooped up and fed well some time
before Christmas. Three days before it is slaughtered it
should have an English walnut forced down its throat three
times a day, a glass of sherry once a day. The meat will be
deliciously tender, and have a fine nutty flavour.

Benjamin Harrison

I do this great roast turkey with a difference – I chop sage,
thyme and garlic, put it under the skin and massage it for 20
minutes, just like a human back. It's beautifully moist and
tastes unbelievable.

Carole Caplin

It took me three weeks to stuff the turkey. I stuffed it
through the beak.

Phyllis Diller

One Christmas, my wife stuffed the turkey and I cooked it.
I kept putting it back in the oven because there seemed to
be blood everywhere, only to find out she'd used a red
berry stuffing. So the bird got horribly overcooked – and
we all got completely tanked waiting for it.

Michael Praed

A menopausal mother and an electric carving knife – not a
good combination.

Jenny Eclair

Behind every turkey there's a knackered housewife.

Jilly Cooper

Most turkeys taste better the day after. My mother's tasted better the day before.

Rita Rudner

The turkey has practically no taste except a dry fibrous flavour reminiscent of warmed–up plaster of Paris and horsehair. The texture is like wet sawdust and the whole vast feathered swindle has the piquancy of a boiled mattress.

William Connor

The Christmas dinner was fairly ghastly … The turkey was passable, but there were no sausages with it, no rolls of bacon and no bread sauce, and the roast potatoes were beige and palely loitering.

Noël Coward

The turkey was OK. But would have been better if the giblets and the plastic bag had been removed before cooking.

Adrian Mole

Eternity is two people and a roast turkey.

James Dent

What's the difference between a brussel sprout and a bogey? You can't get kids to eat brussel sprouts.

Anon

Ice lay hidden in the green of the Brussel sprouts that we gathered for dinner.

George Sturt

I cannot resist ordering Brussel sprouts every day. The words are so lovely to say.

J. M. Barrie

Talking Turkey

When I was about six I received the following letter from Father Christmas on Christmas Day: 'If you don't eat your greens I shall not be coming next year.'

John Paxton

The most hated vegetable in the land? Tell that to the good folk of Diss in Norfolk whose 6,600 residents buy 54,000 sprouts a week – 75 times the national average. That compares with a paltry 720 in West Bromwich in the Midlands – the sprout-hating capital of Britain.

Lisa Jones

Gary Rhodes wants you to strain your gravy through muslin. As an alternative to spilling it over your shirt and salvaging what you can off the kitchen floor, maybe.

Joe Joseph

A proper Christmas – one that Dickens would approve of – demands fruit cake. Although fruit cakes are the target of many jokes (writer Calvin Trillin, for example, contends that only one fruit cake exists in the world and it simply is passed, unopened, from one fruit cake hater to the next) …

Allison Engel

My first attempt at cooking was a Christmas cake, made in Domestic Science and carried home proudly. I'd iced it with smooth white icing and painted a picture of the three kings on top of it. But I'd omitted to put any glycerine in the icing and it set like concrete. Parental pride turned first to amusement and then to fury as my father, unable to cut the thing, called for a hammer and hammered his thumb and then proceeded to split my mother's favourite bone-handled knife by using it as a chisel.

Pru Leith

Talking Turkey

The Trappist monks at Our Lady of Guadalupe Abbey in Lafayette, Oregon, produce a dark, heavy fruit cake that is studded with pecan halves, chopped walnuts and candied cherries, and flavoured with 120-proof brandy. The cake has little in common with the light, flour-filled commercial varieties, and as Father Paschal Phillips ... put it: 'When you slice our fruit cake and hold it up to the light, it looks like stained glass.'

Allison Engel

... that crisp white icing which crunches like frozen snow, and that essential layer of amber marzipan before the rich innards of the old English Christmas cake are reached.

Godfrey Smith

Alcohol was significantly present in my mother's Christmas cake. It was the speciality of the house. Essentially a fruit cake, the ingredients had been soaked in rum, brandy or port for weeks. That was obvious from the first bite ... I have always been grateful that my mother's cakes reached their alcoholic apogee before the age of the breathalyser.

Sir Trevor McDonald

Best Cishmash Cake Reshippy

Ingredients:

1 cup butter	1 teaspoon baking soda
1 cup sugar	1 tablespoon lemon juice
4 large eggs	1 cup brown sugar
1 cup dried fruit	1 cup nuts
1 teaspoon baking powder	1 or 2 quarts of aged whisky

Before you start, sample the whisky to check for quality. Good, ain't it? Now go ahead. Select a large mixing bowl, measuring cup, etc. Check the whisky again as it must be just right. To be sure the whisky is of the highest quality, pour 1 level cup into a glass and drink as fast as you can.

Repeat.

With an eclectic mixer, beat 1 cup of butter in a large fluffy bowl. Add 1 teaspoon of sugar and beat the hell out of it again. Meanwhile, at this parsnicular point in time, wake sure the whixy hasn't gone bad while you weren't looking. Open second quart ifnestessary. Add 2 large leggs, 2 cups fried druit an' beat 'til high. If druit gets shtuck in peaters, just pry the monsters loosh with a drewscriver.

Example the whikstey again, shecking confistancy, then shitf 2 cups of salt or destergent or whatever is in preach. Chample the whitchy shum more. Shift in shum lemon zhoosh. Fold in chopped sputter and shrained nuts.

Add 100 babblespoons of brown booger or whushever's closhest and mix well. Greash ubben and turn the cakey pan to 350 decrees. Now pour the whole mesh into the washin' machine and set on sinsh shycle.

Check dat whixny wunsh more and pash out.

Anon

I hate fruit cake because it sticks to the knife when you cut it and breaks when you try to pick it up and whatever you do pick up sticks to all your fingers together and each finger separately. And then sticks to your lips so they stick together for hours afterward ...

Jim Quinn

A number of other truly remarkable things show up in holiday dinners, such as ... pies made out of something called 'mince', although if anyone has ever seen a mince in its natural state he did not live to tell about it.

P. J. O'Rourke

I walked home again with great pleasure, and there dined by my wife's bed-side with great content, having a mess of brave plum-porridge and a roasted pullet for dinner, and I sent for a mince pie abroad, my wife not being well to make any herself yet.

Samuel Pepys, Diary, 25 December, 1662

Up, my wife to the making of Christmas pies all day, and I abroad to several places.

Samuel Pepys

I come from a long line of spectacularly brilliant cooks whose pastry came out golden every time and melted in the mouth. It is not, regrettably, a talent I inherited. So every year it's: 'Mum, why aren't your mince pies as good as Grandma's?'

Jenni Murray

Women used to make great mince pies and fake orgasms. Now we can do orgasms but have to fake mince pies. Is this progress?

Allison Pearson

Like Albion's rich plum-pudding, famous grown,
The mince-pie reigns in realms beyond his own,
Through foreign latitudes his power extends,
And only terminates where eating ends.

William Hone, Ode to the Mince-Pie

Little Jack Horner
sat in a corner,
eating his Christmas pie;
he put in his thumb,
and pulled out a plum,
and said, 'What a good boy am I!'

Nursery rhyme

Talking Turkey

I finally finished the gingerbread man. The last thing I ate was his foot and, you won't believe this, but on the way down my gullet he kicked me.

Groucho Marx

In December, the principal household duty lies in preparing for the creature comforts of those near and dear to us, so as to meet old Christmas with a happy face, a contented mind, and a full larder; and in stoning the plums, washing the currants, cutting the citron, beating the eggs, and mixing the pudding, a housewife is not unworthily greeting the genial season of all good things.

Mrs Isabella Beeton

The general madness sets in with the construction, weeks ago, of the Christmas pudding. The witches in *Macbeth* seem like Cranford figures in comparison with an Englishwoman really throwing herself, so to speak, into her pudding:

> Each ingredient done double
> Fire burn and cauldron bubble
> Someone's colon's in for trouble.

Arthur Marshall

The majority of Christmas puddings demand a huge appetite, iron constitution, indomitable will, sense of humour and dash of Christmas spirit.

Rory Ross

In half a minute Mrs Cratchit entered – flushed, but smiling proudly – with the pudding, like a speckled cannon-ball, so hard and firm, blazing in half of half a quartern of ignited brandy, and bedight with Christmas holly stuck into the top.

Charles Dickens, A Christmas Carol

Talking Turkey

Oh, a wonderful pudding! Bob Cratchit said, and calmly too, that he regarded it as the greatest success achieved by Mrs Cratchit since their marriage. Mrs Cratchit said that now the weight was off her mind, she would confess that she had had her doubts about the quantity of flour.

Charles Dickens, A Christmas Carol

The plum-pudding was of the same handsome roundness as ever, and came in with the symbolic blue flames around it, as if it had been heroically snatched from the nether fires, into which it had been thrown by dyspeptic Puritans.

George Eliot, The Mill on the Floss

I had observed Shackleton ferreting about in his bundle, out of which he presently produced a spare sock. Stored away in that sock was a small round object about the size of a cricket ball, which when brought to light, proved to be a noble plum pudding. Another dive into his lucky-bag and out came a crumpled piece of artificial holly. Heated in the cocoa, our plum pudding was soon steaming hot, and stood on the cooker-lid crowned with its decoration. Our Christmas Day had proved a delightful break in an otherwise uninterrupted spell of semi-starvation. Some days elapsed before its pleasing effects wore off.

Captain Robert Falcon Scott, Christmas Day 1902, during his unsuccessful attempt to reach the South Pole

What I genuinely loved was Mother's Christmas pudding made from Grandma Quest's recipe. It was thick and gooey and fruity, with little bits of carrot in it, and it clung to your teeth and the roof of your mouth as though showing off before it was swallowed.

Tom Courtenay

Talking Turkey

Christmas Pudding: festering gobs of adamantine suet that the Brits think of as fun food.

Joe Queenan

Christmas puddings by definition are over-rich, claggy, stomach-battering creations. If they aren't, they aren't Christmas puddings.

Matthew Fort

I love Christmas pudding, particularly if it is sliced and fried in butter the next day! At the end of the meal when you are all flagging, suddenly the lights go off and someone brings through a flaming pudding, it brings another 'wow!' moment.

Clarissa Dickson Wright

One of our Christmas rituals was always 'boiling the sixpences'. This was to sterilize them for incorporation in the pudding, which, in turn, was boiled. To this day, my sister still recycles the same old, now obsolete sixpences, some bearing the profile of King George VI, and spat out or choked on by at least two generations of the Humphries family ... EU purists may prefer to interlard their festive dessert with recently excised credit cards.

Barry Humphries

FOR SALE: Christmas Pudding Charms: sterling silver charms to bring good luck. Potential choking hazard: do not use with food.

Past Times catalogue

Although the so-called tradition of putting money in the pudding isn't really an ancient custom at all, it's just a Yuletide conspiracy dreamed up by orthodontists, who know that coins hidden in food have an unerring ability to locate and crack a weak tooth, thereby enabling emergency dentists to charge quadruple fees on Boxing Day, so they can buy that nice new BMW they've had their eye on all year …

Victor Lewis-Smith

If your pudding is loaded with coins and thimbles etc., then be sure to tell your guests. One year I forgot to mention it and our Vera ended up in casualty. They found a watch, two holy medals and £2.10s.6d in used change in her stomach.

Lily Savage

The table at which the King sat was richly decorated and groaned beneath the good fare placed upon it; for there was brawn, roast beef, venison pasty, pheasants, swan, capons, lampreys, pyke in latimer sauce, custard, partridge, fruit, plovers and a huge plum pudding which required the efforts of two men to carry.

Anonymous account of Henry VIII's Christmas feast at Greenwich, 1486

78,000 Christmas puddings have been given to staff.

Eighty Things About Queen Elizabeth II, 2006

Ah, what an excellent Thing is an English Pudding! 'To come in Pudding time' is as much as to say, to come in the most lucky Moment in the World.

H. Misson, 1719

Grammy Moon's famous plum duff is a pudding boiled in a cloth bag. Grammy Moon had a secret ingredient. She'd soak it for hours in rum, then ignite it in a blinding flash. As soon as she came out of the kitchen with no eyebrows, we knew dessert was ready. To this day, the smell of burning hair puts me in the holiday spirit. Merry Christmas!

Daphne Moon, Frasier

Talking Turkey

Life is like chewing your Christmas pudding really carefully because you are fearful you may be the lucky one with the threepenny bit.

Lynne Truss

Hey kids! I made your favourite cookies: Christmas trees for the girls and bloody spearheads for Bart.

Marge Simpson, The Simpsons

After a good dinner one can forgive anybody, even one's own relatives.

Oscar Wilde

There is a remarkable breakdown of taste and intelligence at Christmastime. Mature, responsible grown men wear neckties made of holly leaves and drink alcoholic beverages with raw egg yolks and cottage cheese in them.

P. J. O'Rourke

Rudolph's red nose is not alcohol–related.

Bart Simpson, writing lines on the blackboard as a punishment,
The Simpsons

You can tell it's the Christmas season. Stores are selling off their expired milk as eggnog.

David Letterman

– The Advocaat doesn't 'arf make me sleepy.
– Does it? Would you like another one Norma?

Nana and Jim Royle, The Royle Family

Eggnogs: Because these lethal concoctions contain a generous measure of what are usually breakfast ingredients, there is a school which holds that a shaker of them is a perfect way to start Boxing Day. The same school probably believes that because crème de menthe tastes of peppermint, it is good for brushing the teeth with.

Keith Waterhouse

Winter is a time when otherwise harmless and pleasant people invite one to parties and serve 'this rather interesting punch Audrey has been brewing up, do try some'. A quick glance around the room on such occasions reveals guests absently poking around the tepid contents of little beakers with the enthusiasm of people unexpectedly called upon to unblock the drains.

Peter Parker

I have heard people blame laced sherry trifle, but this is very unusual.

AA spokesman on Julie Wynn's successful defence that she was driving under the influence of whisky-soaked Christmas cake

> Nor frost, nor snow, nor wind I trow,
> Can hurt me if it would,
> I am so wrapped within and lapped
> With jolly good ale and old.

Anon

Drink will take the place of parlour games and we shall all pull crackers and probably enjoy ourselves enough to warrant at least some of the god–damned fuss.

Noël Coward

… I have something which makes it all bearable, the presents, the in-laws, other people's children, your own children, the games, the noise, the mess, the ridiculous meals. It consists of one part French cooking brandy, one part Irish whiskey and four parts fresh milk. The hard part is remembering to have put milk instead of water into one of your ice trays the previous night. Drink the mixture immediately on rising, while the others are having breakfast or throwing up behind the snowman.

Kingsley Amis

Came home at 3:15, not tight, loosened, if anything, one or two joints unbolted, no more than that, perfectly capable of sticking key in letter-box and walking into Christmas tree.

Alan Coren

Your mom is so full of Christmas cheer and enough tranquillizer to take down an elephant.

Peter Griffin, Family Guy

Popular belief (despite popular experience) has it that there is a hangover amnesty during Christmas. Not so. The liver knows no seasons.

Keith Waterhouse

So let me leave you with this Dickensian remedy for the morning after the night before. It's the inspiration of the great writer's great-grandson Cedric Dickens – the living embodiment of Pickwick himself. Make a well in the centre of a steaming hot bowl of porridge. Fill it with Drambuie, then pour single cream round the bowl. Sprinkle brown sugar all over the top. It's guaranteed to set you up for the new year.

Godfrey Smith

Pull the Other One!
Christmas Crackers

On average, four people a year break their arm pulling a cracker.

Anon

Pulled the Other One!

The perfect way to pull a Christmas cracker

- Tilting your end of the cracker downwards at an inclined angle during the pull
- A firm, two-handed grip to prevent the cracker being torn
- A steady and controlled pull
- The distance to the centre of gravity of the cracker
- The length of the cracker
- Good quality and strong materials used in construction
- Avoid twisting from the shoulder when pulling

QinetiQ, Science and Development Agency, BBC news website

Everyone feels happier for having pulled a cracker. If it were up to me, I would introduce Christmas crackers into every large social gathering, regardless of the time of year.

Craig Brown

My favourite thing is to buy a box of cheap crackers from the supermarket, carefully unpick the ends, tip out the junk inside, then carefully replace each one with a small, personalized gift, such as a tiny photo frame with a picture of their child or spouse inside it. Guests love that.

Amanda Lamb

I've been buying in cheap Christmas crackers, unscrewing them and doctoring the insides with dirty jokes (for the prudes) and appropriate dodgy presents, such as hair restorer for my old man and Viagra for my nan to give to the man in her life.

Jamie Oliver

[*Reading a joke from a cracker*] 'The ooh-aah bird is so called because it lays square eggs.' I don't understand that one.

Margot Leadbetter, The Good Life

Christmas Cracker Jokes

Christmas cracker jokes are just a way of binding people together … If the joke is good and you tell it and it doesn't get a laugh, it's your problem. If the joke's bad and it doesn't get a laugh, then it's the joke's problem. My theory is that it's a way of not embarrassing people at Christmas.

Professor Richard Wiseman

Consumers genuinely prefer corny jokes, we've actually had complaints after trying to introduce more genuinely amusing gags – it seems that the British public have fond memories of groaning at a bad punchline after pulling their crackers!

Julian Reed, Robin Reed cracker manufacturers

No sex, no religion and no politics. What have you got left?

*Evelyn Bishop, head of joke development at the Tom Smith Group,
cracker makers*

The badness of the jokes is part of the Christmas tradition and I would absolutely hate it if anyone tried to modernize them.

Frank Muir

Christmas Cracker Jokes

What is a lawyer's favourite pudding?
Sue it.

What asks no questions but needs answering?
A door bell.

How do you prevent your mouth freezing?
Grit your teeth.

What do you call a man who's been buried for 100 years?
Pete.

Where do fairies go to recover from Christmas?
Elf farms.

What do you call a blind reindeer?
No eye deer.

How do you get holy water?
Boil the hell out of it.

What's yellow and dangerous?
Shark-infested custard.

What do you call a Frenchman wearing sandals?
Felipe Felop.

What goes splash, splash, splash, splash, splash, splash, splash, clop?
An octopus with a wooden leg.

What's large, white and deadly if it falls out of a tree?
A fridge.

Why does Santa have three gardens?
So he can hoe, hoe, hoe.

What do you get when you walk under a friendly cow?
A pat on the head.

What's a dentist's favourite musical instrument?
A tuba toothpaste.

What do you call a group of grandmasters of chess bragging about their games in a hotel lobby?
Chess nuts boasting in an open foyer.

Did you hear about the Irish woodworm who was found dead in a brick?

Christmas Cracker Jokes

Did you hear about the two aerials who got married?
Apparently the reception was brilliant.

A man walks into a bar and says 'ouch'.

What's grey, yellow, grey, yellow, grey, yellow, grey, yellow, grey, yellow?
An elephant rolling down a hill with a daisy in its mouth.

Did you hear about the two ships that collided at sea? One was carrying red paint and the other was carrying blue paint. All the sailors ended up being marooned.

What athlete is warmest in winter?
A long jumper.

What did baby corn say to mummy corn?
Where's popcorn?

What does a fish say when it swims into a concrete wall?
Dam!

How do monkeys make toast?
Stick some bread under the gorilla.

Who hides in the bakery at Christmas?
A mince spy.

What do you get if you eat Christmas decorations?
Tinsilitis.

What do you get if Santa goes down the chimney when a fire is lit?
Crisp Kringle.

Why did the golfer wear an extra pair of trousers?
In case he got a hole in one.

Hark the Herald Angels Sing: Christmas Music

Christmas is coming. In Beverly Hills the carollers are
already going round singing, 'Oh come all ye facelifts …'

Joan Rivers

The Christmas I like has more to do with Pickwick than
the Pope; that's probably why my favourite Christmas song
is 'God Rest Ye Merry Gentlemen', which is a sort of
religious version of 'Roll Out the Barrel'.

Julie Burchill

The great thing about carols is that because you learned
them at school, you can still remember all the words when
you go drunk to Midnight Mass.

Jo Brand

As always for Midnight Mass the place was crowded. The
singing of the choir was somewhat elaborate but
refreshingly vigorous. I spotted that my fly was unzipped
when giving voice to 'Silent Night', a sure sign of advanced
age in the male of the species.

Alec Guinness

Of the hundreds who wrote to me last week complaining
of everything from the price of crackers to carol singers
who only know the first two lines of 'Silent Night', I liked
best the man who said that he understood some people like
everyone else to know they're in church, but that there was

Hark the Herald Angels Sing

absolutely no need for the unseemly competition to see who could sing the last 'O Come Let Us Adore Him' at the highest volume.

Terry Wogan

Why are children performing 'Away in a Manger' in headlong, wondrous rush so much more affecting than in-tune King's College Choir? Dig down into bosky corner of coat pocket and find Kleenex.

Allison Pearson

You know, for years I thought the herald angels were Herod angels. I didn't like to ask how come Herod had angels and why we were singing about them, but now, with 40 Yuletides ebbing behind me, I think my original version was the better.

A. A. Gill

The little Lord Jesus lay down his wee ted.

Frances McMillan

We are not, by and large, a singing people, not since our misguided government axed choral singing in schools, but you can still experience a Cup Final sort of thrill as the Royal Albert Hall resounds to 'O Come, All Ye Faithful' sung by 6,000 voices. Carols as social glue? Why not?

John Rutter

The week before Christmas, when the snow seemed to lie thickest, was the moment for carol singing; and when I think back to those nights it is to the crunch of the snow and to the lights of the lanterns on it.

Laurie Lee, Cider with Rosie

Our house was a singing house during the holidays. Although the boys are getting big for it now, we used to go out – the five of us – singing Christmas carols around the neighbourhood. Those we serenaded asked us in for refreshments, and there were cookies for the youngsters and a few shiny coins for all of us.

Bing Crosby

If we took the same approach to Christmas songs that we take to the language of federal rules and regulations, instead of 'Silent Night', we'd be singing about 'noise-mitigated post-daylight time intervals'.

Al Gore

Least Popular Christmas Carols

- Rudolph the Reindeer with an Inner-Ear Disorder
- Joy to the World Wrestling Federation
- It's Beginning to Look a Lot Infected
- Frosty the Paedophile
- Jack Frost Roasting on a Open Fire
- Walking in a Woman's Wonderbra

David Letterman

Christmas Carols for the Psychiatrically Challenged

- Schizophrenia: Do You Hear What I Hear?
- Multiple Personality Disorder: We Three Queens Disoriented are
- Dementia: I Think I'll be Home for Christmas
- Narcissistic: Hark the Herald Angels Sing About Me
- Manic: Deck the Halls and Walls and House and Lawn and Streets and Stores and Office and Town and Cars and Buses and Trucks and Trees and Fire Hydrants and …
- Paranoid: Santa Claus is Coming to Get Me
- Borderline Personality Disorder: Thoughts of Roasting on an Open Fire

Hark the Herald Angels Sing

- Personality Disorder: You Better Watch Out, I'm Gonna Cry, I'm Gonna Pout, Maybe I'll Tell You Why
- Obsessive Compulsive Disorder: Jingle Bells, Jingle Bells, Jingle Bells, Jingle Bells, Jingle Bells, Jingle Bells, Jingle Bells, Jingle Bells, Jingle Bells ...

Anon

Alternative Christmas Carols

While shepherds watched their flocks by night
all sitting on a bank,
an angel who was bored came down
and taught them how to –
– Merry Christmas, everybody!

Children and Reverend Geraldine Granger, The Vicar of Dibley

We three kings of Leicester Square
Selling pants a penny a pair
How fantastic, no elastic
Falling down everywhere!

Once in Royal David's City
Stood a lowly cattle shed,
Where a mother laid her baby
In a manger for his bed.
Social workers found them there,
And now the little chap's in care.

Good King Wenceslas looked out
From his cabbage garden
Bumped into a brussel sprout
And said 'I beg your pardon.'

Hark the Herald Angels Sing

While shepherds washed their socks by night
All seated round the tub
The angel dropped a packet down
And they began to scrub.
They scrubbed and scrubbed and soon they found
That then their socks got brighter
And still they scrubbed until they found
That Persil washes whiter.

The Twelve STIs of Christmas

On the first day of Christmas my true love gave to me ... a bug that made it hard to pee.

On the second day of Christmas my true love gave to me ... chlamydia, and a chance of infertility.

On the third day of Christmas my true love gave to me ... syphilis, chlamydia, and my testicles are sore and lumpy.

On the fourth day of Christmas my true love gave to me ... genital herpes, syphilis, chlamydia, and a discharge that is hourly.

On the fifth day of Christmas my true love gave to me ... gonorrhoea, genital herpes, syphilis, chlamydia, and the possibility of HIV.

On the sixth day of Christmas my true love gave to me ... pubic lice, gonorrhoea, genital herpes, syphilis, and an infection that was urinary.

On the seventh day of Christmas my true love gave to me ... hepatitis, pubic lice, gonorrhoea, genital herpes, syphilis, chlamydia, and a visit to the surgery.

Hark the Herald Angels Sing

On the eighth day of Christmas my true love gave to me ...
trichomoniasis, hepatitis, pubic lice, gonorrhoea, genital
herpes, syphilis, chlamydia, and my groin itches constantly.

On the ninth day of Christmas my true love gave to me ...
genital warts, trichomoniasis, hepatitis, pubic lice,
gonorrhoea, genital herpes, syphilis, chlamydia, and sores
that spread anally.

On the tenth day of Christmas my true love gave to me ...
scabies, genital warts, trichomoniasis, hepatitis, pubic lice,
gonorrhoea, genital herpes, syphilis, chlamydia, wearing
pants with some difficulty.

On the eleventh day of Christmas my true love gave to me
... pelvic inflammatory disease, scabies, genital warts,
trichomoniasis, hepatitis, pubic lice, gonorrhoea, genital
herpes, syphilis, chlamydia, and I no longer feel horny.

On the twelfth day of Christmas my true love gave to me
... crabs, pelvic inflammatory disease, scabies, genital warts,
trichomoniasis, hepatitis, pubic lice, gonorrhoea, genital
herpes, syphilis, chlamydia, and no one will make love to
me.

*A carol created for a Department of Health website to raise awareness
of the risk of catching sexually transmitted infections*

Tory MP Tim Loughton discovers that the Department
of Health spent £60,000 last Christmas on a website
carol 'The 12 STIs of Christmas'. This included a chorus
of dancing stick figures graphically suffering assorted
sexually transmitted infections and displaying their
inflamed genitals ... Mr Loughton complains: 'It doesn't
even scan!'

The Daily Mail, 2004

Yes, Bob, we do know it's bloody Christmas. There won't be snow in Africa this Christmas? Kilimanjaro – snowy peaks all year round.

Jimmy Carr

Christmas songs help us feel young in spirit, even though we may be older in years.

Norman Vincent Peale

God gave Moses the Ten Commandments and then He gave Irving Berlin … 'White Christmas'.

Philip Roth

Irving Berlin took Christmas, took Christ out of it, and made it about the weather.

Philip Roth

Staying in Palm Springs, Irving Berlin looked back fondly to the white Christmases of his own childhood in New York. He wrote 'White Christmas' over a weekend. On Monday morning he burst into his office declaring, 'Not only is it the best song I ever wrote; it's the best song *anybody* ever wrote.'

Mick Brown

A competitor of Irving Berlin's complained that Berlin has used up all the holidays: 'I'm Dreaming of a White Christmas', 'Easter Parade', and so on.

Groucho Marx

'White Christmas' is a great song with a simple melody … It's as much a part of me as 'When the Blue of the Night', or my floppy ears.

Bing Crosby

Hark the Herald Angels Sing

The song 'White Christmas' is like an old Christmas memory: it inspires a happy sadness in the heart.

Bing Crosby

The song 'White Christmas' still evokes my own Christmas memories. It does, I suppose, because it celebrates more than a holiday – it symbolizes home.

Ronald Reagan

In New York when you hear someone sing, 'You better watch out …' it means there's a mugger behind you.

Joan Rivers

Experts at Music Choice, a digital music channel, analysed all the Christmas Number 1 singles of the past 30 years and identified eleven criteria for success. They included harmony, use of sleigh bells, pealing church bells, children singing, seasonal references to love and nostalgic lyrics. They concluded that Sir Cliff's 1988 hit 'Mistletoe and Wine' was the most perfect Christmas hit, despite no key change for the third verse, no charity involvement, and no use of a novelty front person.

Alan Hamilton

Sir Cliff Richard's songs embody the spirit of a family Christmas: 'Saviour's Day', 'Mistletoe and Wine' and, of course, 'It's So Funny We Don't Talk Anymore'.

Jimmy Carr

We accept Cliff Richard at Christmas, he's part of it. No other time though. Father Christmas in July is annoying and so is Cliff Richard.

Paul Morley

Better an eternity in Hell with Little and Large, Max Bygraves and Dick Emery than a single Christmas with the Osmonds.

Clive James

'Merry Xmas Everybody' is, and always will be, the great British Christmas hit, because it's an unapologetic party song ... The song instantly conjures images of Noddy Holder, frizzy hair exploding from either side of his head like a doodle in the phone book, his fringe obediently plastered to his forehead, or wedged under that ridiculous mirrored top hat. Father Christmas may not exist, but I believe in Noddy Holder.

Andrew Collins

Former glam rocker Roy Wood ... Brum's pagan love-Santa ...

Jonathan Meades

He's Behind You! Christmas Entertainment

– After they've had their dinner they always play charades, y'know, and parlour games.
– Is their telly broke?

Antony and Denise Royle, The Royle Family

After supper we played games – best of all – The Game – where people acted out words, or phrases, given to them by the opposing team. We specialized in book titles ... The funniest one I remember was *Lady Chatterley's Lover* which my mother-in-law had to act out, and I would not have dreamed she had in her what emerged.

Robertson Davies

He's Behind You!

After decorating the tree, I put the girls to bed, send Jamie out of the room, then call him back in, and greet him dressed in nothing but a pair of jingle bells on my boobs, and do a silly dance.

Jools Oliver, wife of celebrity chef Jamie Oliver

This is a wonderful traditional Yuletide game. It's called the Indian Ocean Game. Everybody sits round in a circle, and the first person to mention that the Indian Ocean is forty thousand fathoms deep, loses.

Denise Coffey, Do Not Adjust Your Set

My favourite Christmas party game: take seven large bottles of vodka. Pour them into a bucket or suitable receptacle. Drink. Lie on the floor for several hours. Don't go to bed. Repeat until dead.

Mel Smith

There is probably a smell of roasted chestnuts and other good comfortable things all the time, for we are telling Winter Stories – Ghost Stories, or more shame for us – round the Christmas fire; and we have never stirred, except to draw a little nearer to it.

Charles Dickens

Christmas V Mastermind was not a success. It was also the last of my plays that I appeared in. I played a villain in a dressing gown who pushed a Christmas fairy out of a fifth floor window having fastened her wings together with a bulldog clip. One of the few laughs in the show, I recall. A woman wrote and said, after watching it, she was never coming to our theatre again. Ah, me.

Alan Ayckbourn

He's Behind You!

Advent calendars are all very well if you're a Blue Peter sort of family, but everyone knows that for the rest of us serfs Christmas really begins with that satisfying thump on the doormat or that first glimpse of the glossy piles on the newsagent's counter. Yes, the arrival of the double issue of the *Radio Times*.

Stuart Maconie

While we like to portray a traditional British Christmas as one non-stop hoopla of carol singing, bracing Boxing Day hikes and playing Scrabble in askew paper hats, the reality is rather more sloth-like. Because what we Brits really do is simply watch the telly. Loads of telly. And almost the same telly every year. A word from the Queen at 3 p.m.? *The Two Ronnies* doing their 'four candles' sketch? Double *EastEnders* (featuring at least one death), Del and Rodney, rounded off with a comforting slice of *Morecambe and Wise*? These are our real Christmas traditions.

Grace Dent

Christmas was pleasantly quiet. The most enjoyable half hour was spent watching 'Wallace and Gromit'.

Alec Guinness

'The Snowman' does it for me because this is the supreme Christmas masterpiece of our age. A boy's snowman comes to life and takes him flying over snow-covered fields to a party with Father Christmas where they feast and dance until night ends. Celebrating children, innocent happiness, winter snow, Santa Claus, communal pleasure and the miracle of regeneration when the snow thaws and day replaces night, this has got it all. My wife and I can re-enact the whole thing and used to fly the children, held aloft at arm's length, over the back of the sofa.

Stephen Pile

He's Behind You!

Christmas wouldn't be Christmas without a good dose of misery from the soaps.

Ilona Amos

The annual punch-up at the Queen Vic is as much part of Christmas Day as the Queen's speech.

Jane Warren

Christmas is always a dangerous time in soaps. In *Crossroads* once, Benny climbed up a ladder to put a fairy on the motel tree and never came down. Neither he nor his bobble hat were ever seen again.

Nancy Banks-Smith

Things I Hate About Christmas: The Queen's annual shot at TV stardom. It never gets any more entertaining or less patronizing. Yet the entire day appears to be constructed around it.

Iain Grant

After the ritual exchange of presents, socks for me, lavender water for Hilda, we ate enough to ensure a gentle snooze during the broadcast by Her Majesty the Queen.

John Mortimer, Rumpole of the Bailey

Ten People Least Likely to Appear on Television Dressed as an Impish Christmas Elf in an Advertisement for Asda: 1) Dame Mary Warnock. 2) Leonard Cohen. 3) Gerald Kaufman. 4) Alexander Solzhenitsyn. 5) Dr Ian Paisley. 6) David Blunkett. 7) Harold Pinter. 8) A. S. Byatt. 9) HM the Queen. 10) J.D. Salinger.

Craig Brown

He's Behind You!

Having to review the past two weeks of Christmas television, I feel like the fat, lazy victim on *You are What You Eat* who has been confronted with a table groaning under saturated, oversweetened and processed programmes, with added E-for-entertainment numbers.

A. A. Gill

Where would we be without *The Sound of Music* on television at Christmas?
My house.

Jimmy Carr

At Christmas, boys want to watch *The Great Escape*, girls want to watch *The Sound of Music*. They're actually exactly the same film: in *The Great Escape*, Steve McQueen is escaping from Nazis, and in *The Sound of Music*, Julie Andrews is escaping from Nazis – but she's singing.

Andy Riley

Least Rented Christmas Movies: "'Twas 243 Nights Before Christmas'; 'Frosty, the Anatomically Correct Christmas'; 'The Grinch Who Sold Christmas on eBay'; 'Tiny Tim: Big Where It Counts'.

David Letterman

The nativity play is like chicken pox – it's something we all go through, and leaves us slightly scarred.

Tim Firth

A note from my granddaughter's school was pinned up in my daughter's kitchen a few days ago, which read: 'Alice is an angel. Please can she wear white knickers on Tuesday.'

David Shamash

He's Behind You!

We've been given the parts in the nativity play. And I'm the lobster.

Daisy, Love Actually

In this year's nativity, my niece Lydia will take the role of a blade of grass.

David Ponte

I was a mince pie in our school nativity play.

B. Madgwick

The infants' nativity play, in front of a packed house, is called 'Rock Around the Flock' and has a brisk run through the familiar story, together with ten songs, some more familiar than others. I'd never heard 'If We're Happy and We Know It' sung by angels at Christmas before.

Stephen Bates

For me there's never been one perfect Christmas. It's more a series of snapshots, memories of moments that add up to perfection. They begin with my daughter, Lucy, aged three, at her kindergarten Christmas play, screwing her elfin face into a mask of fierce concentration and bellowing out an ear-splitting solo rendition of 'Little Donkey'.

David Thomas

Rehearsals can prove entertaining ... a soloist insists on singing 'a whale in a manger'.

Maggie Clifford

At Christmas we performed, as did then most junior schools, a nativity play ... I was much amused to see recently than an ambitious performer, envious to shine, and cast in the somewhat dull roll of the Innkeeper, with just one negative response to supply, replied cheerfully when asked whether accommodation was available, 'Oh yes, certainly, please come in,' thus bringing the play to a shorter end than usual.

Arthur Marshall

On Boxing Day we did our panto – huge success. I played Aladdin, and had to run on, crying, 'I am that naughty boy Aladdin whose trousers always need some paddin'!' chased by Alfred as the Widow Twankey in a long curly wig, mob-cap and apron, waving a cane! Alfred and Bertie had a great fight over a roll of cotton-wool for their busts. 'Give me my bust, you swine. You can't have it all, damn you!'

Joan Wyndham

In panto there is a wider variety of pure theatre than you even get in Shakespeare.

Sir Ian McKellen

The pantomime is a Christmas entertainment in the UK, where the leading man is the principal boy who is played by a girl, who romances the leading girl in tights, so that two girls kiss onstage, while the stepmother of the girl is a man in drag, and her two ugly sisters are both men playing women …

Eric Idle

… this bizarre, archetypally British form of entertainment, in which middle-aged men with hairy legs dress up as women and attractive young women in fishnet stockings impersonate lively young men. No wonder we Brits are in such a constant muddle about sex.

Charles Spencer

Pantomime is the smell of oranges and wee-wee.

Arthur Askey

Winter Sports

The smell of wee-wee is still there all right, but these days the fresh and healthy smell of oranges has long gone. It's all crisps now, and giant cardboard cartons of Coke, bars of melting chocolate and great packets of cheap sweets. A colleague with the terrifying task of taking three young children round pantos ... found he had to cope with impressive bouts of projectile vomiting ... as well as the usual umpteen trips to the loo.

Charles Spencer

Winter Sports

Skiing is the only sport where you can spend an arm and a leg to break an arm and a leg.

Henry Beard

There are really only three things to learn in skiing: how to put on your skis, how to slide downhill, and how to walk along the hospital corridor.

Lord Mancroft

Skiing? Why break my leg at 40 degrees below zero when I can fall downstairs at home?

Corey Ford

Skiing strikes me as profoundly un-British. Like Italians playing rugby or the Japanese playing baseball, there is a jarring of cultures which renders the activity risible at best, downright ridiculous at worst.

Stan Hey

The sport of skiing consists of wearing three thousand dollars' worth of clothes and equipment and driving two hundred miles in the snow in order to stand around at a bar and get drunk.

P.J. O'Rourke

If they call it 'downhill skiing', is there an uphill event we don't know about?

Ian Johns

The word slalom means 'slope tracks' and it comes from Norway, like many other commonly used skiing terms including 'oops' (a fall), 'blammo' (a collision with a tree), 'floo' (a bad cold), 'gloop' (food served at a mountain lunch stop), and 'fokkendolt' (a skier who runs into other skiers).

Henry Beard

In St Moritz everyone who is anyone goes around in plaster, which may be fashionable, but is damned uncomfortable. I value my legs as much as Marlene Dietrich values hers.

Noël Coward

I hated skiing or any other sport where there was an ambulance waiting at the bottom of the hill.

Erma Bombeck

A ski jacket is the larval stage of a blimp.

Henry Beard

I now realize that the small hills you see on ski slopes are formed around the bodies of 47-year-olds who tried to learn snowboarding.

Dave Barry

Snowboarding is an activity that is very popular with people who do not feel that regular skiing is lethal enough.

Dave Barry

Winter Sports

And then there's the luge. It takes a perverted mind to come up with a sport which involves inserting yourself into a day-glo prophylactic and hurling yourself down an icy chute on a sledge, with only the muscles normally used in the extremest form of sex controlling your direction.

Stan Hey

We enjoyed Eddie 'The Eagle' Edwards' abject failures because he was, in essence, sending up Alpine sports, in a typically British way. As he plopped off the 90-metre jump with the acceleration of a week-old bread pudding, setting new records for the smallest leap, it was an eloquent raising of two fingers — or two legs in Eddie's case — to Alpine culture.

Stan Hey

Britain doesn't win any medals at the Winter Olympics for one simple reason — we don't have any snow. Now if they had a wet-weather Olympics we would definitely take gold in the twenty-yard dash with a Sainsbury's bag on the head.

A. A. Gill

The only winter sport at which the British excel is phoning in sick.

Ronald White

Rydale is covered with ice, clear as polished steel, I have procured a pair of skates and tomorrow mean to give my body to the wind.

William Wordsworth

An inch of snow fell last night and as we walked to Draycot to skate the snowstorm began again. As we passed Langley Burrell Church we heard the strains of the quadrille band on the ice at Draycot ... The afternoon grew murky and when we began to skate the air was thick with falling snow … The Lancers was beautifully skated. When it grew dark the ice was lighted with Chinese lanterns, and the intense glare of blue, green, and crimson lights and magnesium riband made the whole place as light as day. Then people skated with torches.

Reverend Francis Kilvert

Skating is a chilly pleasure, and therefore, no sin.

Heinrich Heine

… then over the parke (where I first in my life, it being a great frost, did see people sliding with their sckeates, which is a very pretty art) …

Samuel Pepys

The thinner the ice, the more anxious everybody is to see if it will bear.

Josh Billings

I like to skate on the other side of the ice.

Steven Wright

When the cold came before the snow, we went skating on Williams Lake across the Arm. My mother put baked potatoes in the boots of our skates. After the rowboat ferry ride, one oar almost touching the edge of the ice line on the half-frozen Arm, and the walk up to the lake, the skates were warm to put on and the potatoes cool enough to eat.

Robert MacNeil

It always seemed to me hard luck on the very best ice-dancing skaters that they have to spend so much of their time whizzing along backwards, with their bottoms sticking rather undecoratively out.

Arthur Marshall

After the Party's Over

Ice skating is a sport where you talk about sequins, earrings and plunging necklines – and you are talking about the men.

Christine Brennan

After the Party's Over

[*Cheerfully stripping the Christmas tree and binning Christmas cards*] – Well, Christmas is over for another year.
– You could have waited till Boxing Day.

Ben and Susan Harper, My Family

It's Boxing Day and you can't take much more of this … The floor is covered with Big Brother–theme fancy paper from yesterday's orgy of unwrapping. The sofa is strewn with coils of aerosolled spaghetti. The son is inconsolable because some small cousin has walked on his Crash Bandicoot 5 Playstation disk and ruined it … You have had it up to here with tangerines. You are dyspeptic, flatulent, unshaven and grumbling. Much against your wishes, you are gradually turning into Jim Royle.

John Walsh

I forget the derivation of Boxing Day, but the feeling of wanting to invite your loved ones outside one at a time and punch them in the face, does that come into it somewhere?

Allison Pearson

… much like sex, the event ends with a sad flatulent realization that these things are better imagined than enacted, better anticipated than performed.

Stephen Fry

'Twas the day after Christmas,
and all through the house,
the Spirit had ended;
it had all been doused.
The ornaments were yanked from the tree with despair,
while Dad vacuumed pine needles from his rump.

Pete Wrigley, The Adventures of Pete and Pete

Tell-tale signs that Christmas is over

- The kids start playing with their old toys again.
- Television is flooded with holiday ads.
- The biggest queue in M&S is at the exchange counter.
- You get a Christmas card from Australia.
- The house is full of food, but everyone's on a diet.
- You're looking forward to going to work.
- The box of dates is put back in the cupboard for another year.
- It's safe to answer unexpected rings at the door.
- Easter eggs appear in the shops.

You Magazine

The man in the Hoover shop said what is it, needles in the works again?

Alan Coren

Christmas ain't over 'til the fat angel sings!

Anon

The day after Christmas: when we all have two more ugly sweaters.

Craig Kilborn

In London after Christmas you always get the great New Clothes Parades in the parks! Families go out together, and they are all wearing their new Christmas pullovers – even

After the Party's Over

staid old businessmen! I love it. And another thing I like
about this time of year is the smell of damp wool – mittens
and scarves gently steaming on the radiators after wet or
snowy afternoon perambulations.

Thora Hird

In early January friendly Christmas cards continue to
arrive, struggling gamely home like the last few stragglers in
a London marathon.

Arthur Marshall

The day after Christmas and I was doing Christmas cards
for next year for John Loring at Tiffany's ... diamonds with
real diamond dust on it, a set of nine. Each card has part of
the diamond and when you put the nine together it makes
one diamond.

Andy Warhol

– I was determined to have a happy Christmas.
– Did you?
– I think so. I don't remember much, and that's always a
good sign, isn't it?

Evelyn Waugh, Brideshead Revisited

Next to a circus, there ain't nothing that packs up and tears
out any quicker than the Christmas spirit.

Kin Hubbard

So, the season is over, the cards recycled, the refuse men
tipped, the candle wax dug out of the Menorah, the
earrings exchanged for the kitchen clock, the case-on-
wheels and accompanying mother-in-law deposited on a
station platform and the inflatable beds deflated. As are we
all.

Maureen Lipman

After the Party's Over

It being Epiphany we packed up the Christmas cards and put the crib back in its cake tin until next year. A crib? Well, not exactly; the Holy Family, Wise Men and Shepherds all made of small Peruvian gourds and very solemnly painted, all with wide staring eyes.

Alec Guinness

Next to the presidency, detrimming a tree has to be the loneliest job in the world. It has fallen to women for centuries and is considered a skill only they can do, like replacing the roll on the toilet tissue spindle, painting skirting boards, holding a wet washcloth for a child who is throwing up or taking out a splinter with a needle.

Erma Bombeck

The Christmas tree inspires a love/hate relationship. All that time spent selecting and decorating, and a week after, you see it by the side of the road, like a mob hit. A car slows down, a door opens and a tree rolls out. People snap out of Christmas spirit like it was a drunken stupor – 'There's a tree inside the house! Throw it anywhere!'

Jerry Seinfeld

No one loves a Christmas tree on January 1. The wonderful soft branches that the family couldn't wait to get inside to smell have turned into rapiers that jab you. The wonderful blinking lights that Daddy arranged by branch and colour have knotted themselves hopelessly around crumbling brownery and have to be severed with a bread knife. The stockings that hung by the chimney with care are hanging out of sofa cushions, and they smell like clam dip. And the angel that everyone fought to put on top of the tree can only be removed with an extension ladder that is in the garage, and no one can remember how to fit it through the door.

Erma Bombeck

Ring out the old, ring in the new,
Ring, happy bells, across the snow:
The year is going, let him go;
Ring out the false, ring in the true.

Alfred, Lord Tennyson

Christmas Past

— What was Christmas like in the old days?
— Same as it is now. Diabolical to the spirit and remorseless
to the bowels.

Carter Brown and Uncle Mort, Charades with Uncle Mort
by Peter Tinniswood

The idea of Christmas is like a note struck on glass — long
ago and for ever. For each of us, this is the earliest memory
of the soul … The Holy Night links up all childhoods; we
return to our own — to the first music, the first pictures, the
first innocent and mysterious thrill and stir.

Elizabeth Bowen

Christmas is a form of distillation. It is the decoction of
childhood and adult experience, simmered and condensed
like a vial of precious liquid, then sealed in crystal, and
slipped close to the heart.

Margaret Murphy

Christmas is a time for remembering. So that's me f***ed.

Ozzie Osbourne, Dead Ringers spoof

Christmas is sights, especially the sights of Christmas
reflected in the eyes of a child.

William Saroyan

Christmas Past

My best Christmas is a composite of all those I spent between the ages of four and ten at my grandfather's house in Hampshire – opulent, traditional, magical, with Father Christmas and little velvet dresses and tinsel from the tree in your hair. Then my parents split up and I went to a boarding school and it was never the same.

Rose Tremain

Were I a philosopher, I should write a philosophy of toys, showing that nothing else in life needs to be taken seriously, and that Christmas Day in the company of children is one of the few occasions on which men become entirely alive.

Robert Lynd

The best Christmas was the one when I was five, before worldliness and wisdom began to set in.

Charles Kuralt

Christmas is the keeping-place for memories of our innocence.

Joan Mills

The one thing I remember about Christmas was that my father used to take me out in a boat about ten miles offshore on Christmas Day, and I used to have to swim back. Extraordinary. It was a ritual. Mind you, that wasn't the hard part. The difficult bit was getting out of the sack.

John Cleese

There's nothing sadder in this world than to awake on Christmas morning and not be a child.

Erma Bombeck

Every Christmas, I feel like a little child. But we always get turkey.

Terry Jones, Do Not Adjust Your Set

Christmas Past

Christmas to a child is the first terrible proof that to travel hopefully is better than to arrive. It is impossible in adulthood to recapture the same kind of wriggling excitement, clammy anticipation and fidgeting desperation that one felt as the little carboard doors of the advent calendar swung open.

Stephen Fry

It is good to be children sometimes, and never better than at Christmas, when its mighty Founder was a child himself.

Charles Dickens

I do like Christmas, but I don't like all the palaver, the phoniness of it. I like the way it was; three apples and a banana in a little bag and a pair of jeans and a checked shirt which you were told was a cowboy suit.

Tom Murphy

My Christmas wish is that for a little while I might know and live again in the world I knew when I was ten years old.

Paul Gallico

Oh how nice it would be, just for today and tomorrow, to be a little boy of five instead of an ageing playwright of fifty-five and look forward to all the high jinks with passionate excitement and be given a clockwork train with a full set of rails and a tunnel.

Noël Coward

The idea that Christmas is only for children is nonsense. The longer we live, the more Christmas means.

Dorothy Walworth Crowell

Christmas is for children. But it is for grown-ups too. Even if it is a headache, a chore, and a nightmare, it is a period of necessary defrosting of chill and hide-bound hearts.

Lenora Mattingly Weber

For children, Christmas is anticipation. For adults, Christmas is memory.

Eric Sevareid

As you get older, you may think Christmas has changed. It hasn't. It's you who has changed.

Harry Truman

Christmas, in its final essence, is for grown people who have forgotten what children know. Christmas is for whoever is old enough to have denied the unquenchable spirit of man.

Margaret Cousins

Christmas comes but once a year, and when it does it makes you feel *sodding fed-up*, because you remember all the Christmases when you were a child and enjoyed yourself, eating and being given presents and wearing paper hats and being give a sip of Daddy's port.

Kingsley Amis

When we recall Christmas past, we usually find that the simplest things – not the great occasions – give off the greatest glow of happiness.

Bob Hope

At Christmas, no house is childless. Up to the surface wells a forgotten capacity for simplicity, an aptitude and eagerness for delight. The most elderly fingers tremble with expectations as they pluck at knots of tinsel ribbon; wrappings disclose 'surprises' which send a flush up cheeks. The real children wake earlier – that is the only difference!

Elizabeth Bowen

Christmas Future

Which Christmas is the most vivid to me? It's always the next Christmas.

Joanne Woodward

What will Christmas 2074 be like?

- 33 per cent believe that Christmas Day bank holiday will be abolished in 70 years' time, and everyone will be working straight through.
- 43 per cent of us think Christmas crackers will have been banned for health and safety reasons.
- 45 per cent think shopping centres will no longer exist, and we'll all do our shopping on line.
- 10 per cent think Santa will be depicted as a woman.
- 33 per cent think Christmas trees will exist only as holograms, which will be decorated automatically at the flick of a switch.
- 50 per cent of us think Christmas cards will be obsolete, and greetings will all be sent digitally.
- 49 per cent think families will get together via video conference on Christmas Day.
- 12 per cent of us think we'll be eating sushi for Christmas dinner instead of turkey.
- 33 per cent think the Queen's Speech will be abolished and replaced with a 'message to the nation' given by a politician or celebrity.

Quality Street Research

– This snow is beautiful. I'm glad global warming never happened.
– Actually, it did. But thank God nuclear winter cancelled it out.

Philip Fry and Turanga Leela, Futurama

Bah! Humbug! Christmas Scrooges

'A merry Christmas, uncle! God save you!' cried a cheerful voice. It was the voice of Scrooge's nephew ... 'Bah!' said Scrooge. 'Humbug!'

Charles Dickens, A Christmas Carol

Every idiot who goes about with Merry Christmas on his lips should be boiled with his own pudding, and buried with a stake of holly through his heart.

Charles Dickens, A Christmas Carol

Ruddy Tiny Tim, ghastly little toad, complete waste of a perfectly good crutch.

A. A. Gill

... we know the whole Cratchitt Family would be far better off on a ten-day Entrepreneurial Skills development course than getting humiliating handouts.

Peter York

No-ho-ho.

Tagline for 'Christmas with the Kranks', later withdrawn after focus groups objected to its cynical tone

What's Christmas but a time of paying bills without money, a time for finding yourself a year older and not an hour richer etc. Old Ebenezer was not wholly without reason. Though it is not for riches I long, but repose of the soul ...

Robertson Davies

Bah! Humbug!

Like all intelligent people, I greatly dislike Christmas. It revolts me to see a whole nation refrain from music for weeks together in order that every man may rifle his neighbour's pockets under cover of a ghastly pretence of festivity.

George Bernard Shaw

Well, what shall we hang, the holly or each other?

Henry II, The Lion in Winter

Don't talk to me about Christmas, will ya? All that sticky, phoney goodwill. I'd like to get a giant candy bar and beat the wings off a sugar plum fairy.

Oscar Madison, The Odd Couple

Because Christmas is generally accepted as pleasure's pinnacle, the happiest day of the year, it causes widespread and sometimes fatal depression. Many adults look forward to it and its aftermath as to dental surgery …

Barbara Holland, Endangered Pleasures

I am sorry to have to introduce the subject of Christmas … It is an indecent subject; a cruel, gluttonous subject; a drunken, disorderly subject; a wasteful, disastrous subject; a wicked, cadging, lying, filthy, blasphemous, and demoralizing subject.

George Bernard Shaw

The next person says Merry Christmas to me, I'll kill him.

Nora Charles, The Thin Man

Roses are things which Christmas is not a bed of.

Ogden Nash

The collectivization of gaiety and the compulsory infliction of joy.

Christopher Hitchens

Bah! Humbug!

It is really an atrocious institution. We must be gluttonous because it is Christmas. We must be drunken because it is Christmas ... We must buy things that nobody wants and give them to people we don't like; because the mass of the population, including the all-powerful, middle-class tradesman, depends on a week of licence and brigandage, waste and intemperance, to clear off its outstanding liabilities at the end of the year ... As for me, I shall fly from it all tomorrow.

George Bernard Shaw

I have long thought it a pity that Scrooge, like so many people in Dickens, spoilt his case by overstatement. To dismiss the Christmas spirit as humbug will not quite do as it stands, but it gets close.

Kingsley Amis

What's so special about Christmas – the birth of a man who thinks he's a god isn't such a rare event.

Graffiti

There's a universal law: 'Happy people do not need festivity.'

Quentin Crisp

Twelve days of Christmas. One day of Christmas is loathsome enough.

Raymond Shaw, The Manchurian Candidate

– What are the Cranes known for if not their legendary holiday spirit?
– I hate singing and I hate Christmas and I'm going to bed.

Martin and Frasier Crane, Frasier

Bah! Humbug!

It is customarily said that Christmas is done 'for the kids'. Considering how awful Christmas is and how little our society likes children, this must be true.

P. J. O'Rourke

My father was cheap. Every year he'd say, 'I'm glad Christmas comes but once every other year.'

John Roy

My ten favourite things about Christmas: 1) It only comes once a year. 2) It only lasts a day. 3) I can't think of anything else.

Neil, The Young Ones

How to ruin the Christmas Day spirit

- Stay in bed until lunchtime.
- Remind everyone of the calories in a piece of Christmas pudding.
- Read a book while everyone else plays charades.
- Refuse to read out the motto from your cracker because it isn't funny.
- Tell a five-year-old he's too old to believe in Santa Claus.
- Say 'Have you still go the receipt?' when you open your main present.

You Magazine

Christmas is forced on a reluctant and disgusted nation by the shopkeepers and the press: on its own merits it would wither and shrivel in the fiery breath of universal hatred; and anyone who looked back to it would be turned into a pillar of greasy sausages.

George Bernard Shaw

Last week my Mum said to me: 'Tray, it's strange the way you dislike Christmas as much as me. I often wonder if it's hereditary.'

Tracey Emin

I hate Christmas, I hate the silly music on the radio, I hate the adverts. I don't like the mince pies involved.

Noel Gallagher

All this Christmas madness is driving me crazy. I hate the sound of sleigh bells (where in Britain can you see a sleigh in action?) and the fact that thousands of spruce trees are sacrificed to the cause. I abhor the enforced cheerfulness of strangers, and the lunatic jollity of 'Jingle Bells' blaring out of a thousand loudspeakers. I hate Nigella telling me that Christmas in the kitchen doesn't have to be a horror show ...

Debra Craine

Or consider Christmas – could Satan in his most malignant mood have devised a worse combination of graft plus buncombe than the system whereby several hundred million people get a billion or so gifts for which they have no use, and some thousands of shop-clerks die of exhaustion while selling them and every other child in the western world is made ill from overeating – all in the name of the lowly Jesus?

Upton Sinclair

I hate Christmas. Everything is designed for families, romance, warmth, emotion and presents, and if you have no boyfriend, no money, your mother is going out with a missing Portuguese criminal and your friends don't want to be your friend any more, it makes you want to emigrate to a vicious Muslim regime where at least *all* the women are treated like social outcasts.

Bridget Jones, Bridget Jones's Diary

We both hated Christmas. We only did it for the children.

Mrs Irving Berlin

Bah! Humbug!

Something in me resists the calendar expectation of happiness. Merry Christmas yourself! it mutters as it shapes a ghostly grin.

J. B. Priestley

Christmas Day my arse!

Jim Royle, The Royle Family

Given the choice, where would you rather be this Christmas – in your own kitchen with your hand shoved up a turkey's bottom, or somewhere as far away from tinsel, turkey and tree as possible? The classic Great Christmas Escape is simply to tell everyone you're going away, buy a skipload of TV dinners and DVDs, take the phone off the hook, close the curtains … and wake up on 27 December.

Bernice Davison

I hate Christmas … First of all I am an atheist – thank God … The hypocrisy of it all, it is a shopkeeper's delight. I see women who are panicked by the kids into spending money they can't afford on crap that will only be thrown away. The murder rate goes up at Christmas. Most families hate each other and can't wait to say piss off. I had a wonderful Christmas once – in Australia where I swam, had a mammoth breakfast and then read. I yelled out of the window: 'Bah humbug.'

Warren Mitchell

I could never see why people were so happy about Dickens's *A Christmas Carol* because I never had any confidence that Scrooge was going to be different the next day.

Dr Karl Menninger

Bah! Humbug!

This is a day of goodwill to all men, and the giving and receiving of presents which nobody particularly wants, a time for planned gaiety, determined sentiment and irrelevant expense; a religious festival without religion; a commercialized orgy of love without a heart. Ah me! I fear I am becoming cynical, but how lovely it would be if it were an ordinary day on which I could get on with my work and read and play …

Noël Coward

The cure [for Christmas] is to simply ignore it. You have to put up with about four years of disgrace when you receive Christmas cards and do not send them, but after that you know that the people who send you Christmas cards are doing it to please *you* and that they don't expect a reply.

Quentin Crisp

I believed in Christmas until I was eight years old. I had saved up some money carrying ice in Philadelphia, and I was going to buy my mother a copper-bottomed clothes boiler for Christmas. I kept the money hidden in a brown crock in the coal bin. My father found the crock. He did exactly what I would have done in his place. He stole the money. And ever since then I've remembered nobody on Christmas, and I want nobody to remember me.

W. C. Fields

We were never a festive family. My mother still travels on Christmas Day as she gets a free glass of champagne on planes. She once looked after my flat as I escaped to sunnier climes. I rang her guiltily on Christmas Day only to be told that she was blissfully happy, had had a plate of baked beans and hadn't seen anyone all day.

Dom Joly

Bah! Humbug!

I don't do Christmas: I send no cards, I sing no carols, I buy no presents, I eat no turkey. I spend Christmas alone. While the rest of the nation is knee-deep in bread sauce, spent wrapping paper and squealing children, I shall be stretched out on the settee, cat on my lap, toasted cheese sandwich in one hand and the video remote in the other, watching months of missed movies. It's the most relaxing day of my year.

Debra Craine

Cancel the kitchen scraps for lepers and orphans, no more merciful beheadings, and call off Christmas!

Sheriff of Nottingham, Robin Hood, Prince of Thieves

Despite a shared passion for facial hair and redistributing wealth, Papa Castro has never got on with Father Christmas. The Caribbean Scrooge banned the holiday [in Cuba] in 1969 because it interfered with the sugar-beet harvest. It was reinstated in 1997, coincidentally just before the Pope visited Fidel.

Keith Laidlaw

If you're dreaming of a tight Christmas then hotelier Bill Ward may have just the answer. Instead of a day of presents and celebrations centred around a feast of turkey and all the trimmings, Bill is offering simpler fare for those whose gut reaction to the festive season is 'bah humbug'. Bill is turning his Dunsley Hall Country House Hotel, near Whitby in North Yorkshire, into a decoration-free zone for Christmas, with not a sprig of holly in sight. Any mention of turkey will attract a frown and soup and a sandwich will be on the menu for Christmas dinner. Any Scrooge-like guest who has the misfortune to be greeted with a 'Merry Christmas' from a member of staff will be entitled to a £5 gift voucher.

Northern Echo

Maybe people are not as miserable as we thought.

Bill Ward, hotelier, reporting no bookings so far for his Scrooge holidays for people who want a Christmas-free break

We Wish You a Merry Christmas! Christmas Greetings

I wish you an Abi Titmus and a Happy New Year.

Richard Curtis

May your Christmas be full of friends and booze and no shocks.

Philip Oakes

Merry Stressmas.

Anon

A crappy isthmus and a preposterous New Year ...
Christmas is a time of peace and good willy to all men ...

Doctor Roger Smith, President of the Loyal Pismonunciation Society (Ronnie Barker)

Meritricious and a Happy New Year.

Gore Vidal

Forgive us our christmases as we forgive them that christmus against us.

Samuel Butler

We Wish You a Merry Christmas!

Knowing me, knowing Yule Ah-haa.

Alan Partridge

A fruity, flatulent Christmas.

A. A. Gill

Merry Christmas, movie house! Merry Christmas, Emporium! Merry Christmas, you wonderful old Building and Loan!

George Bailey, A Wonderful Life

A Merry Christmas to all my friends except two.

W. C. Fields

The charming aspect of Christmas is the fact that it expresses goodwill in a cheerful, happy, benevolent, non-sacrificial way. One says 'Merry Christmas' – not 'Weep and Repent.' And the goodwill is expressed in a material, earthly form – by giving presents to one's friends or by sending them cards in token of remembrance …

Ayn Rand

It is my heart-warmed and world-embracing Christmas hope and aspiration that all of us, the high, the low, the rich, the poor, the admired, the despised, the loved, the hated, the civilized, the savage (every man and brother of us all throughout the whole earth), may eventually be gathered together in a heaven of everlasting rest and peace and bliss, except the inventor of the telephone.

Mark Twain

Have Yourself a Merry Little Christmas.

Ralph Blane, song title

We Wish You a Merry Christmas!

A Merry Christmas to us all. Eat, drink and be merry, for this time next year Ebenezer Brown may be in charge.

Mick Hume

'God bless us every one,' said Tiny Tim, the last of all.

Charles Dickens, A Christmas Carol

Index

Index

Index

Index

Index

Index

Index

Index

Index